Ruby Langford Ginibi was born at the Box Ridge Mission, Coraki, on the north coast of New South Wales in 1934. She was raised in Bonalbo and went to high school in Casino where she finished second form. At age fifteen she moved to Sydney and qualified as a clothing machinist. Her first child was born when she was seventeen. She has a family of nine children and raised them mostly by herself. For many years she lived in tin huts and camped in the bush around Coonabarabran, working at fencing, burning off, lopping and ring-barking, and pegging roo skins. At other times she lived in the Koori areas of Sydney and worked in clothing factories. She is the grandmother of twenty children. Her autobiography *Don't Take Your Love to Town* was published in 1988.

Also by Ruby Langford Ginibi

Don't Take Your Love to Town

REAL DEADLY

RUBY LANGFORD GINIBI

Angus&Robertson
An imprint of HarperCollins*Publishers*

AN ANGUS & ROBERTSON BOOK
An imprint of HarperCollinsPublishers

First published in Australia in 1992 by
CollinsAngus&Robertson Publishers Pty Limited (ACN 009 913 517)
A division of HarperCollinsPublishers (Australia) Pty Limited
25-31 Ryde Road, Pymble NSW 2073, Australia
HarperCollinsPublishers (New Zealand) Limited
31 View Road, Glenfield, Auckland 10, New Zealand
HarperCollinsPublishers Limited
77-85 Fulham Palace Road, London W6 8JB, United Kingdom

National Library of Australia
Cataloguing-in-Publication data:

Langford, Ruby, 1934-
    Real Deadly.

    ISBN 0 207 17421 0

    1. Langford, Ruby, 1934-. [2] Aborigines, Australian—Women—
    Biography. [3]. Aborigines, Australian—Social life and customs. I.
    Title

994.0049915

Cover photograph of Ruby Langford Ginibi by Pam Johnston
Typeset in Australia by Midland Typesetters, Maryborough, Victoria
Printed in Australia by Griffin Press

5 4 3 2 1
96 95 94 93 92

ACKNOWLEDGEMENTS

Sections from Koori Days first appeared in *Heroines*, edited by Dale Spender (Penguin 1991).
'Taxi Conversations' by Aileen Corpus appeared in *The Penguin Book of Australian Women Poets* (Penguin, 1988)

Contents

ODE TO THE RICHMOND RIVER AND THE BUNDJALUNG PEOPLE

You were a source of abundant food for my people the Bundjalung tribes. Your shores, Bungawalbyn, Jackabulbyn, Minumi, Coraki, Gibberagee, all surrounded by a place known as the big scrub—plenty bush tucker around, bunihny, binging, burbi.

No more do warriors hunt and bring home nunghing so that our family clans can eat. Gone are all our tribal ways, only three elders left; all dubays, no old nugthungs, to tell our stories and legends or give us our laws. No more corroborees, no more singin', no more clap sticks, no more bullroarer tellin' of initiation, no more diggin' for yams with yam sticks. Only broken-down homes, with paint peelin' and fences fallin' down and cars to go to town in on pension and endowment days for shopping.

A basketball court, where once a garden grew; only little hall for land council meetings, where they sit and argue about no funds to lift our living standards up. No more mission school! bus come to take 'em into town school; not allowed in, long time ago; lot of changes since time long gone, some good, some bad! No jobs around for bagal or dubays or jarjums too, now the place has been colonised and settled.

Only boredom, unemployment and poverty, and drinkin' white man's booze! Big landowners, that dispossessed them of the land, and everything! Livin' in mansions on the hills, away from the flood reaches of the old Richmond River, selling Murray Grey cattle to live in affluence while the Bundjalung people, who worked and built up those big cattle stations, as cooks, stockmen, housemaids and servants survive in a time warp, livin' in fourth world conditions, in poverty compared to the affluence of THE MANSIONS ON THE HILLS!

NOTES

bunihny: porcupine	*nugthung:* grandfather
binging: turtle	*dubay:* woman
burbi: koala	*nunghing:* tucker
jarjums: children	

KOORI DUBAYS 1

My Mother: she gave birth to me!
26 January, 1934

My recollections of my mother are from when I was a little girl; her voice softly telling me that when I was a baby she used only Palmolive soap on my skin because that kept it smooth and soft. And because I was the eldest of the three girls in her marriage with Dad, I was prompted to ask, 'What about Gwennie and Rita? What soap did you use on them?'

'Well,' she said, 'Gwen was a Lux soap baby, and Rita, the youngest, was a Palmolive girl just like you.' That ended my childhood curiosity for a little while, and pleased me greatly. For I thought . . . Rita and I are dark, and Gwennie is real fair, and I wondered if that had anything to do with the selection of the soaps, because everyone knows that Palmolive is a dark soap, but that Lux is white! You see, I was a very questioning child, a 'stickybeaky kid', and I wanted to know it all. There were other things too that I had a burning desire to know. Boy, what a stickybeak I was.

And I listened in great wonder. When my mother would tell me about the olden times when they used to travel in real old buses to dances in different towns. That in those days the dances were olden-time dances, and they had an MC who made them all form a circle, and when the music started up they all moved off together and became one swirling mass of dancers. The music was played on an old button accordian and gum leaves, a guitar, an old violin and a mouth organ. Hurricane lamps hung on nails at vantage points around the hall, giving the old wooden place a soft warm glow.

3

I remember some of the dances too. There was the Pride of Erin, waltzes, quicksteps, and the progressive barn dance. And the old sets. We kids were allowed to dance inside the circle so the grown ups couldn't tread on us. We were only little you see.

I remember the Master of Ceremonies and another bloke, standing at the back of the hall and giving a rendition of,

Oh Mr Gallagher, and Mr Sheen . . .

You're the biggest, ugliest 'B' I've ever seen . . .

And they would sing these ditties back and forth, insulting each other amid much laughter from all the dancers.

Gwennie and I won a pair of spoons for our dancing. We were good little dancers too. And there'd be big open fires lit out the back of the hall, with women bustling round making tea and cocoa, and slicing up damper to eat. It was a very happy atmosphere.

Then on the way going home, how sleepy Gwennie and me would be; so sleepy that Mum and Dad bedded us down in the port racks on the bus, with a blanket and a pillow under our heads. And that's where we stayed, snuggled up, until we reached home. I remember the bus's motor humming, and people singing; it made us real contented as we nodded off to sleep.

Going back in my thoughts, I can recall Mum searching for bush tucker, for bunihny and binging. How she would take us kids to a swamp, and settle us down while she got into the water, tucking her dress up into her bloomers and then wading around feeling with her feet until she got a binging and wrung its neck, killing it. Then she'd throw it onto the bank where me and Gwennie waited with a chaff bag to put them into.

Back at home a fire was lit in the old fuel stove. She'd lay the turtles on their backs to cook inside the oven while we waited patiently for a good feed. Other times she got us bunya nuts from the bunya pine trees and broke them up with a tommy axe and roasted them for us in the hot coals. They were good tucker too. Filled our little bellies up.

All these memories are of a long time ago. I didn't have much chance to get to know her well, my mother. Because she ran away and left us on the mission and I was too young to understand why.

We never saw her again until we moved to Sydney. By then we were teenagers. She'd had another family to the man she had run away with. She worked hard and raised that family properly. Although she never raised us, her own children to Dad. My two sisters never forgave her. She died and there was only me and her other children there to mourn her. But I loved her because she gave me life. She brought me into this world and I did love her for that. She always called me *my girl* and she'll always be a heroine in my eyes. And I do know that my father was terribly heartbroken when she left, but that old hurt healed itself, because they became friends before she died.

Mother Nell: she raised me, 1944

After Mum left us, people sent word to Dad who worked in the scrub timber-getting. He knew the old Abo Protection Board would take us and put us in a home to be trained as servants to white people, so he took us three girls back into the bush with him. While he worked we were looked after by Uncle Ernie Ord, tribal doctor and clever man; he caught bush tucker for us, made ashes damper, and told us stories of all the bush animals and birds. He gave me my totem because I was the eldest: willy wagtail. He said it would tell me good news, or bad; it was my messenger bird and would watch and warn me.

Dad took us to live in Bonalbo with his brother, Uncle Sam and his wife, Aunt Nell. The first time I saw her I knew I would love her. She was a big robust woman who wore an apron with a notepad and clothes pegs in the pockets. The pad was for writing shopping lists, and the pegs, for pegging clothes on the line.

I was eight years old and I tried to be just like her. Mother

Nell, we called her, this gracious, kind woman. And she and her husband Sam never referred to each other as Nell and Sam, only as Mother and Father. And she was ten years older than him. But I never heard them argue, never.

She taught me how to milk a cow, and how to crack a horse whip; how to cook, and how to make home-made butter. She also taught me how to love and respect my elders. And not to talk at the meal table—only grown-ups talked at the table.

She taught me the magic of listening to Old Jack Sperring's dance band on Thursday nights; she taught me how to whistle the cows up. She taught us how to laugh, and love; and how to be humble.

If I had ever had the choice of a mother, she would have won the toss.

Mother Nell had one child to father Sam, called Judy. She was a change of life baby, and Mother Nell ended up with a tumour in her stomach. She wasted away to nothing but I'll always remember her laughter and her love because she raised me to be what I am.

In my mind's eye, when things get too much for me, I remember this big robust woman, and feel ashamed of my petty whinges. I feel honoured to have known and shared a piece of her life with her.

I went home to Bonalbo in 1986 for a school reunion. Me, and my two sisters, and Mother Nell's other daughter, Shirley. And we went to our old street, where our old house used to be. But there was not a thing left of the old house. Just all the memories we'd shared with Mother Nell. We walked sadly away, with our memories in our hearts.

THE LEGEND OF DIRRANGUN

I remember being told these stories on the mission at Coraki when I was little. Uncle Ernie Ord had a little hessian bag shack, with a few pieces of galvanised iron for the roof to keep out the rain. He lived in the backyard of the house on the mission where we lived. At night time he would have an old fire bucket that he used for cooking alight, and me and my two sisters who were only little would fight to sit on his lap to listen to his stories about the bush animals and legends. He told me Dirrangun was a witch woman who was always nasty and cranky! He told me that we must never use her name because it was jung to use her name or say it out loud; only the elders could speak her name, though now the legends are being told it's okay to speak these words.

Uncle Ernie said that she lived up in the big scrub that was known as Tooloom and she was very jealous of her son-in-law named Bulagun, and because she didn't like him she hid the drinking water by sitting on the spring. When she wasn't there she covered it with vines and leaves so no one could touch her water. All the tribe went looking for water because they were very thirsty, but she was so nasty that she kept it hidden; one day the water came up out of the spring, and she held it back with her body. The force of the water was so great that she moved her right leg and the Clarence River was formed. The water was getting harder to control and hold back so she opened her left leg and the Richmond River flowed from under that leg. Pretty soon the force of the water carried her out to sea screaming because she was so nasty.

The Clarence and the Richmond both run into the sea at Ballina and Yamba. The Bundjalung territories extend from the Clarence River right up to Ipswich and Beaudesert in Queensland, then down the other side of the Great Dividing Range and all the way back to Grafton on the Clarence River. So this legend was told to me when I was about six years old by Uncle Ernie Ord, wuyan-gali.

NOTES
Bulagun: handsome, young hero
jung: bad
wuyan-gali: clever man

AT BONALBO

In 1944 we lived in Bonalbo in an old outer station house. It had been left to the Hinnett family by the owners of Bonalbo station, because the Hinnetts had given the owners many years of loyal service, as stockmen, housemaids, and servants in general. The owners were the first settlers to come to Gidabal country, which was named after one of the tribal clan dialects of the Bundjalung people.

We kids were bought to Bonalbo to live with our father's brother who had married into the Hinnett family. His wife was a lovely, robust woman we called Mother Nell. Matter of fact, we never referred to either of them as uncle or aunt. They were called just Father Sam and Mother Nell. This was how we referred to them, and how they referred to each other.

We had four or five dairy cows which it was my place to milk each morning and afternoon. Then I used to turn them out of the yard to graze around the town, until I got home from school. Then I'd have to round them up for milking again. All the vegetable scraps and peels were kept in a bucket, for the cows, and it was my sister Gwennie's job to feed the scraps of vegetables to them. We had a gate that swung on hinges, so the cows couldn't get into the gardens beside the house. If they did we'd have no vegetables. One day Gwennie was taking the scraps out to give to the cows and she must have been daydreaming. She forgot to throw the scraps over the fence and she didn't realise this until she was in the yard with the cows. They saw the bucket and knew there was a feed to be had and so ran towards Gwennie. Instead of dropping the damn bucket and running away, she ran with it, holding it in front of her. The cows were pursuing her around and around the yard and she was screaming out 'Mother Nell, Mother Nell, help! help!'

The cows were still chasing her for the bucket when Mother Nell heard the cries for help and looked through the kitchen window. She saw what was going on and called out to Gwennie 'drop the bucket, drop the bucket Gwennie'. She did so, just making it inside the swinging gate with the cows hot on her heels. There was much laughter from Mother Nell and us kids at the kitchen window. Gwennie never lived that down for many years.

HORSY STORY

In 1944, we were the only Kooris living in my hometown of Bonalbo. The family over the back of us, whose backyard ran parallel to ours, were the Browns and our name was Anderson.

They had a blonde four-year-old girl and we had a four-year-old too! She was black but they were both the same age, both named Judy and they were the greatest little friends.

At one time Duncan Brown, Judy's father, kept his racehorse—a long, slim-legged animal—in the backyard of their house. One night he took the racehorse out and replaced it with his draught horse.

Next morning the two Judys had their noses pressed against the fence, looking at the draught horse, with very puzzled looks on their little faces. Judy Brown said, 'He was only little and skinny yesterday.'

'Yeah,' said Judy Anderson, 'but didn't he grew-ed since last night!'

Us bigger kids who overheard them ran around the corner of the house so the littlies couldn't see us burstin' out giggling.

Hurtful Taunts

GIN! BOONG! ABO! COON!

These are the words I had to put up with every day while at school—children's hurtful taunts—my child's mind couldn't understand why. Why do they hate me so? because my skin is black, but we all bleed red! so what's the difference? I hurt and cry and so do they, yet why do they taunt me so?

GIN! BOONG! ABO! COON!

Sticks and stones may break my bones, but names will never hurt me!

GIN! BOONG! ABO! COON!

Christ said, 'Forgive them for they know not what they do.'

But they do know!

Koori Dubays 2

Mum Ruby Leslie: she helped me, 1950

When I was seventeen and having my first child, this lady was to be my baby's grandmother. I wasn't married to her son though. I left Sydney (and the rag trade, where I had learnt my trade) and went to live in Coonabarabran until I had the baby. It wasn't just because I was unmarried and pregnant that I left Sydney. In those days unmarried, pregnant women were looked upon as tarts. And I knew I wasn't one of those. I left because I didn't want to embarrass my dad. He was a dear father to us girls.

His last words to me were, 'If it doesn't work out, Ruby, you come right back here.' I was young, and very inexperienced about most of the facts of life—partly because it was a taboo subject when I was a girl; you didn't even talk about menstruation in front of men.

Mum Ruby was an old hand at having babies. She was one of 'the stolen generation' who had been put into Cootamundra, and it was to her I turned with all my questions about pregnancy. 'How will I know when it is time to go to the hospital?' I would ask her. 'Well,' she replied, 'you'll get these real bad pains, like backache, and they'll get harder and harder to bear until you'll feel like you want to push down and give birth. It takes hours though, OK?' I found this information a blessing as I didn't know a damn thing about child-birth. But Mum Ruby knew. She'd had seven kids of her own.

Her family lived with her and her second husband in a tin shack on the Gunnedah Hill, in Coonabarabran behind the mission. There were several Kooris living in these fringe dwelling camps on the hill, with exotic names—like French's Forest. And where Mum Ruby lived they called 'Leslie's Leap' or 'Leslie's Lookout'. We sure had deadly names for our shanty towns.

I ended up having four children born in Coonabarabran and no matter where I was, Mum Ruby came. Even when I was out in the bush working at ringbarking, or burning off. And she always took the rest of my kids and looked after them when it was time for me to go into hospital for my next birth.

Mum Ruby has a special place in my heart, because she taught me to have strength, and a will to win, and not to let anything beat me. She also taught me how to swing a (kelly) axe, and chop down trees which were then left to dry out for the winter fires. She taught me how to make a bough shed to shade us from the summer heat; how to cook in an old camp oven the best rabbit stews—and how to set the rabbit traps to catch them with.

I could ramble on and on about this old girl, with her smoke-dried hair from the open fires. She was quite a lady. And I'll always be thankful for everything she taught me about life and giving birth. I'm her namesake, Ruby.

Neddy Pearl: my best mate of 37 years, 1950

While I was living on the Gunnedah Hill, Mum Ruby introduced me to Nerida Chatfield, who was one of the Koori women who lived in a tin shanty at the foot of the hill. It was right where the well was that supplied our drinking water. She had ten kids, and she was ten years older than me, and we became firm friends. When my eldest son Bill was born, she was the only visitor I had. She came into the ward with a hand-crocheted bonnet and bootie set, all done in blue, for my little son. He was so small—only weighing 6lb 1oz—and she had to remake the bonnet to fit his head.

Billy's head was the butt of many a joke when he grew into a big teenager. Back in those days he called Neddy his pin-up girl, but I lost Bill when he turned eighteen. He drowned in eight inches of water having an epileptic seizure. And eight months before I buried his sister, Pearl. That was in 1969 and 1970. And Neddy Pearl still has that big safety pin that Bill pinned on her jumper when he christened her his pin-up girl, twenty years ago.

For eleven years I lived in Coonabarabran and did bush work. After I came to Sydney to live in 1962, Neddy's and my roads crossed many times over the years. When I started to write my autobiography in 1984—finishing it in 1987— Neddy played a starring role in it. Because we shared many adventures in life together as 'titis' (sisters); we even shared our boyfriends.

We nursed each other through our grief over the death of our kids. Neddy lost four. I lost three.

I love her just like she was one of my sisters. All the sorrows and joys we shared. We will grow old together, and still be best mates.

Neddy nearly lost her arm when she had a run-in with a train. As she was about to board, it moved, throwing her between the tracks and almost cutting her arm off.

All her family have gone their own way in life. She used to live down the south coast, but she's moved over to Fairfield Heights now, which is not so far away from me. So we'll be able to get together, just like the old days. And reminisce about old times, and all the happiness we shared. We won't look back with anger at our losses but will go forward with hope, and laughter—because that's all we had to begin with.

THE AWAKENING

I came to the city of Sydney when I was a teenage girl to find employment. I can't begin to tell you how many obstacles there were to overcome—you see I was a country girl born and bred, and besides that I was an Aboriginal to boot!

This great city that us country folk referred to as the big smoke was awe-inspiring to me. The year was 1949, and in those years there was a huge push of my people coming to the city to find work, because there was no employment in the country towns. There were great droves of us, trying to get away from the clutches of the Aborigines' Protection Board, who had been rounding my people up like cattle and putting them on to missions.

There you either slaved your guts out for the white manager, or lived on handouts of sugar, tea and flour. Though these missions had enough acreage to run sheep or cattle or grow crops, nothing was done by the Government to implement this. Besides the racism was a terrific burden to bear continually, though white Australia knows little of what my people had to put up with on account of the so-called Protection Act. Some don't even want to know.

I became a clothing machinist, and learned to make shirts, trousers and overalls. There were not many places we Aboriginals could go to without running into nasty, prejudiced people. There was a picture theatre called the Lawson, in Lawson Street, Redfern; there was a blackout there every Saturday night, meaning it was full of us Aboriginal people there to enjoy the movies, and the other meeting place was of a Sunday in Redfern park where the all blacks football team played.

As the years rolled on I went back and forward between

the bush and the city. I had a family of nine children; I had four goes at finding that elusive thing called love and the only good thing I got from these four unions was my kids. I applied for a housing commission home to raise them in (and then I waited ten years for that!) after dragging them from pillar to post, trying to keep a roof over their heads. When I did get the housing commission home, boy! all the dramas—you had to fight to establish yourself there. It was the Government's policy of assimilation, which meant putting us Abos in amongst white people to see if we could live together, though it was a form of cultural genocide.

As the children grew up and went their own ways in life, I moved back into the city, because Green Valley where we lived was a long way out. I was lonely for my people, and there was only me and my youngest son left, but he took up spray painting and it wasn't long before he flew the coop! I moved out to the outer suburbs again and took up residence in an old style boarding house called the Heritage. It was only for Aboriginal people, the first of its kind, and it was home to about ten of us. You had to be able to see to yourself, it wasn't a nursing home. We were co-ed here, boys and girls, only we were older boys and girls. We had twenty-four hour a day staff; WOW! things were sure lookin' up, weren't they!

I'd been on my own for many years now and as a matter of fact I'd given up looking; I was frightened of getting hurt again, but always lived in hope that I might get lucky one day and find someone to share my lonely life with. At this boarding house, the men sat at one table and the women at another. There was this big fella who was an out-of-work actor who had worked in 'A Country Practice', and a few others. He always wore a cowboy hat with feathers in it and was always sneaking glances at me when I wasn't looking. He used to smile nicely to me whenever we passed each other, which caused this lonely old woman's heart to flutter a little. 'Settle down! settle down!' I said to myself.

There was this woman who came to visit him and I thought to myself, well he's taken up, she must be his woman. After I'd gotten to know him better I asked him about her. 'I don't want her, she can't cook and keep a house, I want her to sign her house over to me and I'll kick her out!' I thought to myself you old bastard!

One day I got a call from my son asking for a loan of some money. I offered this big man petrol money to run me over to St Marys. He said, 'Okay, I'll drive you out there.' When we got to St Marys I gave my son the money but we ended up having a row because I was sick of lending him money you see.

I broke down and cried when I got into the car—I felt like an idiot—so the big man took me for a ride in the bush, to forget my sorrows for a while. My eyes took in the countryside that I loved. There were bush flowers everywhere, gum nuts and eucalypts and they all had perfumes all their own. I stooped to pick some and crushed the eucalypts in my hand, and smelled the aroma. 'Beautiful' I said to him. 'Smell this,' and as he did and when our eyes met, it seemed like I became mesmerised. Suddenly his arms entwined me, drawing me close. He pressed his lips to mine, my heart raced madly and I felt like I was being elevated to a higher level. I reached up and put my arms around his neck and nuzzled my face into his beard, the beard I'd been longing to touch for so long.

'Come over here into the bushes,' he said, taking my hand to lead me.

'No,' I said, 'not like this, not yet, my heart's still racing, you took me by surprise!'

'You want to come into the bushes with me don't you? It's what you want, isn't it?' he said.

'Yes', I answered. 'Do you know how long it's been since I've had a man's arms around me, and lips on mine?'

'How long?' he asked.

'Five years,' I said.

'Oh that's not long, I thought you were gonna say ten or fifteen years,' he replied.

'That's too bloody long for me! You should have let sleeping dogs lie—you shouldn't have woken me up! I don't know how to handle it!' I exclaimed.

He kissed me more passionately than before, stirring up the woman in me that had been asleep for so long, so long! I knew that he was waiting eagerly for that walk in the bushes with me, and I was blushing like a little girl, just like I'd never known a man. I wanted so very much to say, 'Yes, yes,' but I couldn't get the words out. I said, 'I'll take a rain check okay, another time—I'm not ready yet.'

'Well don't leave it too long, I can't wait forever!'

We sat side by side in the car on the way home, lost in our own private thoughts. I could see his disappointment and I wondered if he could sense mine too. All that night back home at the Heritage, I tossed and turned, the desire for him burning in my insides. I made myself a vow before I nodded off to sleep. I'll tell him tomorrow, 'Yes yes yes, I need you and want you badly! Say when and I'm all yours.'

Alas tomorrow came and as usual, I was stuck for the words to say to him. All the while I held my head down so he couldn't see my eyes, because if he did, he'd know what was in my heart. All day when I came in contact with him, I was stuck for words. 'Damn,' I said to myself, 'why did he have to wake up all those feelings in me?' That part of my life was finished, but no—here were those feelings that made me blush to the roots of my hair, every time I let myself remember how it was out there in the bush. Desire, passions, sexual arousal and sexual fulfilment were things I hadn't had to think about, I'd gotten so used to being on my own. I'd given up hope of ever finding someone just for me! It's funny, because all I'd ever wanted in life was a workin' man, and all I got was the bums. I know what it's like to be used and discarded like an old shoe.

I'd made this silent vow that never again, never again would I let anyone get close enough to hurt me like that. It seems that I'd built a wall around myself, but in just a few seconds all my defences were shattered, just by this man asking me to go into the bushes with him. 'DAMN HIM!'

Later I'd found out that this old bastard had been knocking off the poor unfortunate woman that hangs around the hostel waiting for him. She hangs around waiting for him to even give her the time of day. She's been with him since her teens and now she's thirty-three. I feel so sorry for her. Her aunt had her tubes tied, so she couldn't have any babies, how cruel. And she wants so badly to have a baby to this sixty-year-old big noter! She's had a reversal of the tubal ligation, so she can fall pregnant to him and he just sits and ignores her and treats her like she's a piece of shit. He eats his meals without even lookin' at her.

I thought to myself, 'You old bastard, she's good enough for you when you're drunk and lookin' for a quick fuck!' I know because she's a nice little woman, and she unburdened her troubles to me there, just needing someone to talk too, because he doesn't.

I thought he was such a nice person—just goes to show you that first impressions can be very wrong.

Four other staff women also said he'd put the hard word on them too! After a good think about this, I could see that this man, if you could call him that, had utterly no respect for women whatever. Who did he think he was? Heaven's gift to all the women of the world? The more I thought about it, the angrier I became. He'd been treating us women like we were proper tarts! The gall of the thing! Here I was swooning over his propositioning of me—why, it would have been like jumping from the frying pan into the fire! Here was this person who called himself a man, with all those using qualities that I detested for so long!

This is definitely what I don't want out of life. I've had all the users I'm going to have, and didn't want or need any more of the same. All those feelings that I'd pushed to the back of my mind needn't surface any more, because

I wasn't about to jump into bed or the bushes with anyone any more. Until I was sure, so damn sure, I'd make my own happiness without the help of any more users.

CRYING TIME

Not to be able to remember or recall what it was like to be in love or loved is very sad; sad also for love to be so painful, that the very essence of it is pushed to the back of one's mind forever, lost in a void of mystery and broken promises.

Although you think to yourself 'sometimes I wish I could recapture that lost feeling' and once again embark on a journey into the senses; to touch, to hold, to fondle, to kiss and embrace, to walk with arms entwined, listening to birds singing their own love songs. Alas, where has my youth gone? Devoured in the daily chores of surviving and putting bread on the table for my hungry brood. The endless struggle to get on top of every situation and hold everyone else up, when most times I feel like crumbling.

Where do I get this spirit from? Is it handed down through the generations from my great spiritual ancestors? It's a great reserve that I have to lean on, every time things get too much for me. But I do believe, that one day there will be someone out there just for me. Someone to lean on and be there when it's crying time, but most of all just be there, when nothing seems to go right. Someone to share sorrows and joy too, and most of all, someone to laugh at life with!

Nobby

A long time ago, in the fifties, I had a big family; though now as the years roll on I have only six of my family left living after nine normal, healthy deliveries; and another nine that no one else wanted, though they were some mothers' sons, the latter ones I'd picked up on my journey through life. This story is about Nobby, my eldest son now, although he was the fourth child in my family in order of birth.

His father was a white man, who I had three jarjums with in my search for that elusive thing called love; I had four of these romantic unions, though none of them lasted the distance—only lasting long enough to bless me with the nine children. The bearing of my kids after all was the most important thing that had ever happened to me.

By the seventies I was a tenant of a housing commission home at Green Valley, an outer suburb of Liverpool, and after all the moving around I finally had a home for my brood and I was overjoyed. These homes out in the suburbs were evidence of the Government's policies of assimilation, which meant that us urban Kooris were put in these housing estates, like Green Valley and Mt Druitt. The idea was to turn us into Europeans with black skins because the image of Australia is 'white'. The only real Aborigines are the tribal ones out in the desert sitting on a rock! Those of us with a degree of caste have never been defined as real Aborigines by the governments of this country.

I lasted there eight going on nine years, and in that time there were so many dramas to overcome, I sometimes thought I was banging my head against the bloody wall trying to cope with all the hardships and racism we had to put up with. If it wasn't the kids fighting then it was the neighbours dobbing you into the damn housing commission—I wondered if it would ever end. I'd lost my two eldest children within eight months of each other in 1969–1970. Me and the kids were looking to start a new life here, and trying to forget the sorrow of the loss of those two kids, Billy and Pearl.

Nobby was my eldest son then and my eldest girl Dianne had married and was living in Eveleigh Street, Redfern. Nobby stayed there to try and get some work. He was only seventeen years old and with two other teenagers he'd gotten drunk and asked one of them to drive him home to me and the rest of the family in Green Valley. (He'd had a row with his girlfriend, because he had caught her out with another bloke.) What he didn't know was that the teenagers had a gun under the seat, and when the teenager was driving negligently the police chased them. The girl in the back started to shoot at the police. Nobby was as drunk as a skunk and was hanging out the front passenger side of the car. When they were caught the teenage girl went crown witness, saying that Nobby was firing the gun—because the police promised to be lenient with her because they needed a conviction, and besides the girl was only fourteen. The other boy was sixteen and Nobby was just seventeen and a bit, but a convenient scapegoat for the police nevertheless. When I visited him in the police cells before court, this son of mine could hardly see out of both of his eyes as the police had bashed him mercilessly. I cried when I saw him and demanded to know who'd done this, and the bastards of police just laughed at me saying he'd fallen over a fence when they chased him. Anyhow, I fronted court for three days of his committal hearing and couldn't go no more because it knocked the guts out of me.

This was the first of a sequence of jail terms in my son's life. Black people have no justice in this country now, let alone way back then in the seventies. He served six years of a ten-year sentence for something he never did, and when he came out in December 1978 he found employment and stayed out of trouble for many years. He became a courier and got on top of things, got a $58,000 home loan from the St George Building Society and purchased a home out in the western suburbs. He found a lady who had two children and proceeded to try and live a reasonably contented life, with as he said, 'everything in the garden lovely'. But the powers that be and the great spirit forces decided he needed a bit more drama to mould him and throw him into more turmoil, stretching him to the limits. My other son David, the father of two children, died of a drug overdose after his missus left him, splitting their little family up. Nobby was inconsolable! He cried out at the funeral, 'Not him! Not him! Why couldn't God take me? I'm the crim! I'm the crim, not him!' These two sons of mine were very close. I used to call them 'the long and the short of it', because Nobby was six feet tall and Dave was about five feet five. When David was drunk he'd say to me, 'Gee Mum, why couldn't ya make me big and tall like Nobby instead of little and black!' and I'd answer, 'There! there! I'm only little and black and I need one of yous to be like me!' and he'd walk away smiling to himself, pleased about that.

They had their differences but there was always a strong bond between them. David would show up sometimes with his little overnight bag saying 'I'm E-victed again Mum' every time he and Debbie would have a row. Nobby used to laugh saying, 'That's married life bra eh!' Then they'd take off to the pub to play pool, or ogle some dubays. They were a great pair those two sons. I remember taking them once to a football match in which the baby son of the family was playing, and these two were running up and down the sidelines yelling out to Jeffery telling him what to do. 'Pass the ball out Jeffo,' they'd call and poor Jeffo said at half-time, 'Mum, tell 'em two to go home, they got me running around silly with all their barrackin' and yellin', they're confusin' me mar.'

I scolded the two of them, huntin' them home so Jeffo could get on with his game. Little did I know that these two rogues used to get the young fella Jeffo in their cars and teach him how to drive—and he was only eight years old at the time!

When Nobby was in jail he'd write these deadly letters to Jeffo encouraging him with his football, sayin', 'When I come home bra, I'll teach ya to play like Ray Price, eh, but don't ya get into any trouble like me or I'll kick ya bloody arse!' He was always encouragin' the young fella, though when he did come home I don't think he ever saw the goalposts of a football field except only on the damn tele, though there were other pressing things he had to take care of, like keeping out of the way of the gungabuls. He was real paranoid about police. If he saw a cops' car coming, he'd watch it until it was way out of sight but that's what jail does to people; I knew he'd be watchin' his back all his damn life, because of the jail terms he'd done.

His life reminded me a lot of my own—the tensions and dramas, and let-downs and heartbreaks; every time he got knocked down in life he was like me, he got up and dusted himself off, and he'd start all over again. Though I used to worry, because there's a limit to the amount of knockdowns you can suffer in this life. It's a good thing he was strong, he had to be!

Another time I was living in St Peters, just across the road from Camdenville Oval. Jeffo had a motorbike and because he was thirteen and had no licence, he used to sneak it into the oval through a hole in the fence and go joy-riding around in there. One day Nobby came over half-charged (he'd had a few beers under his belt), so Jeffery offered him a double on the back of the bike. Nobby boasted that he could handle a bike better than Jeffo but he didn't know that Jeffo had a big ramp made inside the oval. They circled a couple of times and then at full speed Jeffo took him over the ramp. It was a fifteen-foot drop and I could hear Nobby cooeein' from right over the other side of the oval. He jumped off the bike, lettin' out with all these obscenities: 'Ya bloody little mongrel Jeffo, I'm never gonna git on the damn bike with ya again, ya little shitty-arse kid, NEVER AGAIN!' I was out the front of our place bustin' a gut laughin' at them, cause Nobby was sober when he came inside.

There was another time Nobby and David had a row down behind the Clifton Hotel in Redfern. I was staying in at my daughter Dianne's place for the weekend in the early eighties, when one of our relations came tearing up to Eveleigh Street to Dianne's place saying 'ya better come quick, ya boys Nobby and David are killin' each other down behind the Clifton', so I jumped in her car, and me in my nightie and dressing-gown too! When we rounded the corner into the driveway of the Clifton, my two sons were circling each other. Nobby had his feet wide apart so he could be on the same level as David, the short-arsed one; soon as I stepped out of the car they turned to see who it was. 'Hold it! hold it Dave! Not in front of Mum,' Nobby said, waving his arms in the air, and that was the end to the great fight. It seems that Nobby had taken a hammer and knocked all the windows out of Dave's HR Holden and that's what they were blueing about.

A lot of people had gathered around and next thing the cops' paddy-waggon turned the corner and pulled up near them. David was whisperin' under his breath, 'Piss off Nobb, piss off quick, the gungies are comin'.'

With that Nobby said, standin' close to Dave, 'I'm not goin! If they pinch ya they pinch me.'

'What's goin' on here?' the police asked.

'While I was inside at the disco,' David said, 'somebody smashed the windows of me car!'

'Yeah,' Nobby echoed, 'some rotten mongrel did it.'

I had to cover my mouth with my hands to stop from burstin' out gigglin' in front of the gungies. It didn't take them long to stick up for each other when the odds were against them.

At one time my tribal brother Jim Golden was sentenced to four months in Parramatta Jail for driving whilst disqualified. This jail was where Nobby was serving the last part of that ten-year sentence. I got this letter from Jim saying: 'Maude baby, Nobby got me put in his cell here, and he feeds and drinks me like a king; I call him long tack.' So he looked after his old uncle while he was in the can—matter of fact James was the only father-figure my kids ever had. James was always there talkin' to the white man's courts for my boys, though we could never win, because we were faced with white laws, white police, white judges and white juries, and were stuffed to begin with. No equality there, eh!

After David died Nobby went to pieces. We looked for him several times and found him sleepin' it off on David's grave; he was so distressed at his loss he took to driving his courier truck while he was drinkin' and ended up running up the arse of another car. He went back to jail for drunken driving and lost his licence; he had to pay back about nineteen hundred dollars' worth of damages to the other car owner and even had to walk to work. What a comedown! He lost his home when he couldn't meet the last few payments. His lady took off when he was in jail and sold off the home, never giving him any of the funds from the sale, though it was his working ability that got the home loan in the first place. He ended up going and staying with his sister Aileen in Bidwell in the western suburbs. He got on his feet again and saved enough money to buy a little 'bomb car'; lookin' for a bit of lovin' he went up the Cross to get the services of a pro, who robbed him and ran inside the brothel and phoned the police, saying he'd threatened her. This was a bit stupid because he had never had to threaten any of the other women he'd had for sexual pleasures—matter of fact he practically had to beat them off with a stick. He went to trial and fought the charge, but if you can go down, getting convicted on the evidence of a prostitute who had a known criminal record for thievery, you can go down on any charge! He's incarcerated again in her Majesty's brutal prison system that never, ever has listened to Aboriginal pleas, laws or customs.

Nobby's been in jail for over three years now, and most of it has been spent in Long Bay Jail. He waited eight months for a classification so he could go to Berrima Jail to finish his sentence; I go to visit him with my adopted girl who has encouraged him to take up art, and lo and behold I really think he's at last found his forte! Art is the only thing that keeps him going in there and he's promised me he will come out with an arts degree. He has had to go through all this trauma to find his 'real Aboriginal spirit' because it shows in his paintings.

In March 1989 at the Artspace Gallery in Surry Hills they held the first ever Koori Perspecta of art, and Nobby's art was displayed along with a number of Koori works there. Me and most of the family went to see this exhibition. When I did I searched for Nobby's work and found it in the corner. I pulled a big chair into the middle of the room to get a good view. Nobby's painting depicted two black hands tied together with white handcuffs, with blood dripping down from them. Underneath there were dreaming tracks; next to it was a painting which showed a missionary in a long, black gown holding a bible, and a mission truck full of screaming children driving away with their mothers running after the truck crying. I looked at the next one painted by Pammy, my adopted girl, and it showed all these black bodies hanging dead from a chandelier. The caption underneath said, 'What do you call five blackfellas hanging in a prison cell?' The answer was 'A black mobile'. I turned my head around and looked from Nobby's painting to Pammy's on the end. It suddenly hit me in the guts, what I was lookin' at! I burst out crying and my family ran over to see what was up with me. I said: 'Look! There's our history right there in front of us, there's the missionary and the children being taken away with their mothers running after the mission truck. Then Nobby's painting shows deaths in custody, jail, police brutality, the lot and Pammy's shows them hanging in the cells!' I wailed with the kids trying to comfort me; I was so devastated I had the kids get me two or three glasses of white wine to steady me as I was shaking with outrage, at what colonialism and dispossession had done to our race of people. 'Who gave them the damn right to do

29

this to another race of human beings, WHO?' I was thinking it will probably take us another 200 years to pull ourselves out of the shit that has been created for us. All in the name of colonising a land that belonged eternally to the Aboriginal people. I'd been studying up on our Koori history for nigh on seven years and all the injustices we have had to contend with made me so damn angry that I just had to get right away from the typewriter and not write anything for days and days. I know anger doesn't solve anything but it's very frustrating to feel like your hands are forever tied. You feel you can't do anything and are quite POWERLESS to do a damn thing!

This son of mine was definitely a product of his environment, and a victim of circumstances to boot. He also had an identity crisis. I remember when he was only about two, I'd taken him shopping in Coonabarabran where I lived a long time ago. Us Koori people would congregate and sit yarning under the trees in the middle of the streets when they'd come from the mission seven miles out of town; or over on the Gunnedah Hill where a big mob of my people were camped in shantytown huts, made up of scantling offcuts from the saw mills, and hessian bags, or old kerosene tins gotten from the town depot and opened up and beaten down flat with a hammer and nailed to the side walls of these huts. These people couldn't believe that he was my son, because he had platinum blonde hair and was real white! But his father's white and I'm the only black connection he's got to his culture, and today he proudly says, 'I'm a black man wrapped up in white skin.' He often calls himself 'this little black duck', which was one of his brother David's favourite sayings.

At this jail, there's a German art teacher who he thinks is a real deadly artist; this fella calls him 'arsehole' in a joking kind of way or 'Linzzzth' because he lisps a lot when he talks. Nobby has changed his name by deed poll to try and get away from police verbals; I told him that I was gonna disown him because I gave him the name of Gordan but I won't—he is the only one of my kids that has never had the chance to live free from the brutal jail system in this country. And I might add that I never stop worrying about him, though I never go to visit him with a sad face. I always go in there 'laughing like a clown' because I will never let him see the tears that I have shed for him, because it really breaks my heart to see my son behind bars like an animal. This is the only sore point in my life now, though I know in my own way that he's had to go back to that place he calls a 'shit-hole' to find his real Koori spirit and he has found it because it shows in all the art work he has done—because it's all spiritual stuff.

Years ago when I lived in Green Valley I told my kids that one day if we ever won some money in the lottery we'd buy some acres of land and we'd build a place called 'the melting pot' and it would be a place where all the mob could come when they were on holidays and the grandkids could have a couple of horses to ride; and I'd have chooks, ducks and geese, grow my own vegies and have a couple of milking cows for milk for the jarjums. So this was our dream.

I've been back to the mission where I was born after a forty-eight-year absence to find my roots, and with the kind permission of the tribal elders we're gonna establish an art school there to lift the kids up. They need something like this because there's a lot of petty crime, and they have no jobs or anything to do; and I can educate them about the culture of our people because nothing is taught in the schools about our history. And the police are sitting down up there and giving the punishment of these young offenders back to the elders of the tribe; and who better to educate them about the children's homes, boys' homes and the jails than Nobby, who's spent most of his growing-up years incarcerated in them. When his sentence is finished we are Bundjalung country bound, Nobby, Pammy, Patrick, my other adopted son, Allo, and me, because we're gonna pool our resources and finances to make this become a reality, and it will be a new beginning for all of us. And we'll make our own 'dreaming' in the land of my ancestors' Dreamtime!

NOTES
gungabuls: police
jarjums: children

VERBALLED AGAIN

You were a victim of circumstances my son,
I knew you never fired that damn gun,
but because you were the eldest of the three,
that is the way the police said it should be.
A conviction was needed for this case,
so they grabbed you the eldest and slammed shut the gate.
Those cold prison walls were to be your home.
Six long, lonely years you had to roam,
for something you didn't do or say.
Our cries for justice will be heard one day,
when white authorities and the powers that be,
take off the blinkers and really see
all the wrongs they've done to thee.

MAX SILVER

A long time ago I had a son named William Henry, though he was mostly called Bill; he wanted to become a drummer-boy and he pestered and pestered me until I took out a hire-purchase agreement for him to get those 'damned' pearl-based drums. But who could teach him? Who?

At that time our only Koori band based here in Sydney was called the 'Silver-linings'. I remember they were all decked out in these deadly silver suits once at a concert to raise funds for our first hostel for our Koori youth, called Kiniarri. This concert was held in Hyde Park; it was called the Waratah festival and was sponsored by the 2SM good guys of radio. From the stage there was our star footballer of the time Larpa Stewart kicking free footballs out into the audience; also there were Koori models modelling clothes. My girl Pearl was one of them and so was Sue Bryant. They collected over $4,000 in donated funds for Kiniarri.

Afterwards my daughter Pearl took me into a big tent that the *Sun-Herald* paper had, with all the most outstanding photos taken that year in the newspapers. There was a huge photo of Pearl dancing with the Prime Minister John Gorton; and next to her was the photo of Lionel Rose with his hands clasped above his head in victory, after his win over Fighting Harada of Japan for the world title. We ran from this tent, because people were starting to recognise her, and were pointing at the photograph. Those were precious, happy years.

Max Silver was also one of the original Silver-linings band; he played drums and sang too! My son Bill asked him if he'd come home to our place and teach him the basics of drum playing. So the pearl-based drums were set up in my backyard, and every week Max could be seen heading down the lane to our place. I knew it was time to plug me ears with cotton wool, because the whole laneway would rebound with 'fingle-bunt' or 'wipe-out' boy! Did they have some sessions those two, Max and my Billy.

A lot of water has gone under the bridge since then; Pearl died in December 1969, after being hit by a van while she was walking along the footpath. And my Bill died eight months after, in August 1970. He was an epileptic ya see and he drowned in about eight inches of water whilst washing his trousers. He'd taken a seizure and that's where I found him. I gave him mouth to mouth resuscitation and pumped his stomach but he was gone, he was blue-lipped.

Then a few years ago Max, our 'black magic man of music', died of a heart attack. After many years of devoting his music to his people, his band was now called 'Black Lace'; there wasn't a football presentation or a Koori cabaret where he didn't play. I sometimes called him 'The Black Credence Clearwater', too! In my anguished state over the deaths of my two kids, I'd call out 'Max, play Bad Moon Risin', for me Bud!', or play 'Midnight Special', and I'd be cryin' into my beer, very drunk; another time I was at the BIG E, a pub that was our Koori meetin' place in the sixties in Redfern, and the Koori band only had bass guitar and treble, and no bass drums. Us poor blackfellas had nothin'. When in my fogged state I remembered the drums, I said, 'Here's the keys to my place Max, go and get my Bill's drums! They're sitting in the corner there, no Bill to play 'em now.'

'Thanks mum Ruby, thanks,' he called out, going to fetch them. They came back with the drums, set them up and pretty soon the BIG E was rockin' again. I knew in my own heart that my Bill would have been pleased. Ya see in 1984 I buried my other son David, twenty-eight years old and the father of two little kids. He died due to a drug overdose too. So I know what sorrow is and just about a year after Max died, his daughter, a beautiful seventeen year old, overdosed on rohyphnol. Later on three more Koori teenagers, two of the Dumas' girls, died. I knew their mother

Chickee for years, she was so distraught! What is happening to our people? If it's not drugs it's the booze! That's killing us all! We have gotta walk away from these 'white man-made substances' that are killing our young kids and reach back into our Aboriginal culture to get back our heritage and our DREAMING that was taken away from us through the westernisation, imperialism and colonisation of our lands since 1788.

And in my mind's eye I can still see Max, with the little beret he always wore placed cockily on one side of his head, belting out the All Blacks football song 'We keep the ball in motion, just like a rollin' ocean, All Blacks play the game; we keep the forwards busy until their heads get dizzy, All Blacks play the game; and if the others play a little dirty, we'll just do the same, we keep the ball in motion just like a rollin' ocean, All Blacks play the game'. Or when my brother Kevin who was one of the original All Blacks footballers died, how Max got up to sing at the Cricketers' Hotel in Botany Road, Redfern, saying, 'This song is dedicated to our football brother Kevin Anderson who's left us,' and he gave forth with 'Midnight Special'. It made us all cry in remembrance. He always sang better with a few charges of beer under his belt; as I said these are precious happy memories and all our Sydney Koori organisations will tell you that his passing is a very sad loss to all our Koori people, who have ever had the pleasure of being acquainted with him. Rest in peace, our black brother and black magic music man, and my jarjums too.

Little Big Man

Many years ago I was living in Fitzroy Street, Newtown, around 1967–68 it was. My de facto hubby bought home this short man, who he introduced as Jim Golden. He'd known him way out the back country years ago.

Little was I to know that this meeting would end up with this man becoming my tribal brother. In the ensuing years all of us Kooris' lives seemed to cross or entwine. It was like the great spiritual forces had made it happen this way. We at all times picked each other up, every time we got knocked down in the game of life. I might add that it really wasn't a game to be played for fun, though fun we made of it, every chance we got. It was the only way we could cope with all the battling, sorrow, and hardships that life had to offer us. It taught us how to roll with the punches that life gave us—we got to be pretty expert at this duckin' bit! We had to all pull together to survive! It was just like the song said, 'United we stand, divided we fall, and if our backs should ever be against the wall, we'll be together!' That I think is a pretty damn good description of the way we Koori people are.

The following story is all true. I've said I haven't discovered fiction yet. Though the whole history of white Australia is one of fiction, eh! But this story is written with love and respect for someone I love as much as my own 'real' brothers and sisters.

James Golden had been awarded the military medal for service to his country and they don't give those medals to bums, eh!

After all these years this old quiet achiever was gonna

get an award for his services to our Aboriginal people, WOW! The Sunday before the award-giving ceremony, me and Pammy had visited my son Nobby at Berrima Jail for the day and then continued down to Bateman's Bay later on in the afternoon. It was a good three and a half hour trip and I was wondering why this old bugger had to move so bloody far away from us all. Oh well, we all had our own way to go, eh!

Arriving at about seven o'clock, we booked into the Zorba Motel and later on went up to Ibis Place to visit him. I read the speech out to him to get his okay about it. But he said, 'Cut that bit about the war and all that shit, Maude.'

'Why?' I asked. 'Ya gonna bugger me speech up, if I do that,' I said, exasperated.

'Because a man can't go down the soldiers' club without some damn arsehole askin', "Oh you been in the wars eh? Tell us about it." I get the bloody shits because most of these bludgers never left Australian shores,' he said.

I understood and so cut a few things from the speech to please him. We yarned a bit, then left to get a good night's sleep, cause it had been a long day. Back at the motel, I was glad to hit the sack—gettin' too old to tear around. Couldn't let 'little big man' down though, could I?

Next morning Pammy and I were up, showered, dressed and breakfasted by 9.30. We paid the bill and took a tour around to find a newspaper shop. We drove right out to the water's edge, in a little park, not far away from the soldiers' club where the presentation was gonna be. It was a beautiful place.

At 11.30 we drove down to find a parking place at the club and soon we were joined by my daughter Aileen and her little family. We moseyed into the club and were asked to sign the visitor's book, which we did. Then we climbed the stairs to the auditorium where everything was gonna happen.

James and his family arrived and pretty soon the auditorium was filled with about one hundred people. We all seated ourselves, then the Labor member for that area got up and spoke, thanking everyone for coming. He spoke in great detail about the award James was being given and then I was asked to speak.

I stood up in front of the podium. Usually I don't stand to make my speeches, I sit, making myself comfortable. But for this one I was gonna stand, even if it killed me—he deserved respect.

I began, 'I'm here to have a bit of a yarn about my "tribal brother" James Golden. He was born on Tipperena Mission, outside of Narrabri, New South Wales, in the year 1920. He enlisted in the armed forces in 1939, saw action in Malaya and served his country for six years, three and a half of which was spent in that infamous Changi prison. He was in the 8th Division, which they called the "forgotten 8th", and he's served his people all his life. In this country Aboriginal people have seldom received any recognition for their involvement in any of the wars in which Australia has been involved.

'In 1968–69 I was living with my children in a rented place in Portland Street, Waterloo. James was staying with me for awhile even though he worked over on the North Shore. Sometimes he never had the fares to go to and from, so he'd have to, as we Kooris say, "put the long ones in" and walk all the way. We were all poor and battling cause most of the money earned went to pay the rent and keep the landlord happy!

'James would do the rounds of the charities, mostly St Vinnies'. Sometimes he'd come home carrying a box of tinned food on his shoulders that he'd gotten to help me out with food for my kids. When I moved to Riley Street, Surry Hills, James took a flat in the apartment next door as did my sister-in-law, Brenda Leslie. There was a whole mob of us Kooris there, all one big family. At times we called ourselves the Riley Street gang and we all looked after and cared for each other.

'I had sons in and out of trouble with the law, ever since

my two eldest children died within eight months of each other. James was their uncle and he was the only father-figure they'd ever known. He always fronted with me and talked to the law for them. He was so good at it that I told him many times that he'd missed his real calling in life—he should have been on the bench instead of in front of it, talkin' to the white man's courts. Not that my boys were bad—even way back then you only had to identify yourself as an Aboriginal and that was it! You were gone, either into the boys' homes, or the "Big house". It hasn't changed much, cause our people are still dying in police and prison custody.

'James has worked to lift our people up. He started off going down to Paddy's Markets and the fish markets in the sixties in Sydney, to get fresh fruit and vegies and fish for the families of Eveleigh Street, Redfern. He even trained a few of them in the art of boxing. He's jumped in and copped a few of my haymakers when I've had to deal out punishment to some dickheads. So he knows how to duck, though he never calls me Ruby, which is my name. Maude is what he calls me and it's my second name.

'He has been sick for a long while now, very sick, and so without further ado, I love ya James, so do all my kids. May the good spirit of our "Aboriginal Dreamtime" watch over you forever—Wandargie-way.'

There was much applause and then I said, 'I'd like to read a poem that this old "quiet achiever", who we sometimes called the little big man, wrote. It's entitled "Curlew, tribal death bird".

'I have heard the curlew calling,
I listened with all my being
to its awful mournful wail.
Its screaming, screeching call.

Now this old Koori fella,
wanders up here in the sky;

I have not left you yet my people,
not even passed you by;
for this old Koori fella,
only needs to take a long-earned rest.

You will have life's troubles, my people.
They will not easily pass you by;
so come out here in the open and
scream your lungs out to the sky!

So you will find my loved ones;
this old Koori has not forgotten you.
I will take your life's troubles, and ponder them,
before I hear the curlew's last cry.

I will tell you all, my people,
this old Koori only needs rest!
Through all my life's tribulations,
even while I'm at death's door.

I've called to my great spirit
to fight off the curlew's last call,
and help me with my greatest fight.
To stay here amongst you all,
and help you through life's trials.

That big old curlew bird relented,
and granted me my wish;
to stay amongst my people
to lift them up a bit.

He also left a message
that he was close at hand,
and when he finally calls me,
that! I will understand.

My life's work is not yet finished,
for my people there's more pressing things at hand,
to wrest back our tribal lands from others,
who only hold it on REMAND!'

There was much applause. It was a standing ovation for
the man, who the Kooris had named 'Nundue', uncle Jimmy
Golden.

'Thanks very much for listening to me rambling on.' I
then sat down. Other speakers were heard, and last of all
the Labor member presented James with a letter from the
Prime Minister Mr Hawke and the Minister of Aboriginal
Affairs, Mr Tickner, which was read out. James had his
say and we all adjourned to the dining room across the aisle
to have lunch. The Labor member was paying for all the
invited guests—everyone else had to pay for themselves, which
was a bit slack, I thought. We all tucked into Chinese cuisine
and it filled the empty gaps. Afterwards I had a chance to
speak to James alone before we left. 'Don't leave it too
long before you come down again Maude,' he told me.

'Okay,' I said. 'It's my turn to air-raid now. Look, you
seem to have given up, James. Where's the James I used
to know?'

'They only gave me three months to live Maude, the
doctors,' he said.

'I don't give a damn what they say. You fight this, don't
let it beat ya down!'

'Okay, yeah Maude,' he answered.

'We gotta go now,' I said, kissing and cuddling him.

'Okay Maude,' he answered. 'I love ya mate.'

'We gotta go now, bye,' and we left the club, giving a
friend of mine from a long time ago a lift back to Sydney.
Her daughter had had a breakdown, and she had grandchildren
to care for—gotta look after the kids, eh! We travelled back
to Sydney, dropping her off at West Hoxton Park. We saw
her little grandkids come running to help her out of the

car with her belongings. The father came out carrying a three-month-old baby in his arms. How would they manage without old nanny?

When we arrived home I was so dead beat I said goodnight to Pam, and had a cool shower. I jumped into bed to relax and as I lay dozing on and off, my mind went back to all the things I knew about tribal brother James. He'd told me years ago that when he'd come home from the war, he'd found his white wife shacked up with a new Australian—a 'wog' was his words—so he signed the house over to his three kids of the marriage and left. John, Mary, and Michael, and in all the ensuing years he'd never seen hide nor hair of them. I remember once, in the seventies, he was driving me into the city and he took me and showed me the home. The door was open and he knocked, hoping to say hello. I was standing beside him and he wanted to introduce me. But as the door opened, she saw who it was and slammed the door shut right in his face! He jumped back! 'Looks like she never forgave ya for catchin' her with another man,' I said.

He just laughed and said, 'That's all she was good at anyway.' We drove off, with him blowing the horn real loud, BEEP! BEEP! BEEP!

I chuckled to myself, remembering another time when we lived over in Ultimo and his second wife had shoved off with another man. Though she was a Koori, she'd run off with a white man. I used to think that he was about as lucky as me with his love life. Anyhow, she'd left him with two children, little girls they were, and he couldn't work, because of looking after them. I'd first met him when my fourth de facto hubby Lance brought him home. It seemed they were old mates from the bush, though it turned out that my man was one of his wife's ex-lovers. Boy! What a mix-up, eh! James asked me to look after the girls until he could send them back to their tribal granny in Coonamble. It took him two weeks to save the money up, after going back to work in the big woolsheds over there in Ultimo.

One time he took my David to march with him in the big Anzac march, to show him what to do. He'd always told me that when he died his medals were mine, for my kids to march in remembrance of him. I thought that this was real deadly, as this old soldier had the Military Medal, and others for his involvement in the war. I was real proud that he'd asked this of my kids and so were they. He and I made this pact a long time ago, and at the award dinner I reminded him of his promise. He replied, 'Yes Maude, they are your medals, that's stated in my will.'

'Thank ya my brother,' I said. 'That's all I want from you mate.'

That was in 1968 when I lived in 2 Fitzroy Street, Newtown. This was the place where I'd paid a ten-dollar fine of his out of my kids' endowment, so he could go back to work and support his kids. And there was the time when we had no gas at Fitzroy Street to cook our Christmas dinner. He heard of this and sent someone to bring me and all my kids and tita Neddy, with all our Christmas tucker, packed in boxes, while Lance went and took care of the liquid refreshments. There were ten chickens to stuff with seasoning, a leg of pickled pork to be boiled, and vegetables to be baked. My eldest girls Pearl and Dianne rushed around cleaning the house up while me and Neddy stuffed and sewed the chickens before baking them. We were deadly workers and although we hadn't started cooking until eleven o'clock, Christmas dinner was on the table by two o'clock. We were real choppy, eh! The men were in the lounge room sharing a flagon of wine and getting merry with Christmas cheer.

A lot of water has gone under the bridge since then. Another time we lived in Portland Street, Waterloo. It was in 1969. Neddy, James and tita Gert all started calling each other after the movie stars; Neddy was Connie Francis, Gert was Priscilla Presley and James was James Cagney. I was Shirley Bassey and these were times we used to drink to drown our sorrows. We had nothing but each other for comfort in this sad world of ours and we thought it would always be that way. But today Gert's a Christian, no drinkin' or smokin'; Neddy had a fight with a train, and nearly lost her arm, so the train won; and James is an old quiet achiever, getting recognition from the big shots in Canberra—though Mr Hawke or Mr Tickner never fronted to give him that award as they probably had better things to do than give awards to deserving blacks!

While I lay thinking and reminiscing about a time long gone by, I was still chuckling about some of the humorous antics that us mob seemed to get caught up in. I remember James would sit on the floor, beating out a rhythm, singin', 'Do-wana-nun a rarby widingay, Do-wana-nun a rarby widingay, ima-gana ima-gaina ima-agyna who! Do-wana-nuna rarby widingay!' He was singin' about the mating of an emu and a kangaroo. The emu tapped the kangaroo on the shoulder and said, 'You are not of my meat.' All this was beaten out on an old empty beer carton and then all my kids would join in singin'. I used to think sometimes that I'd have to get the hell out of this place.

Another time I remembered a birthday of mine lasting six days. This was when we lived out the valley—Green Valley that is—in the seventies, him and old Shortie, his little mate who he shared a house up in Mt Pritchard with. He came and picked me and Neddy up and took us out to Wallacia for lunch and some champagne on my birthday. I remembered that when we were driving back to Green Valley that night, James was so pissed that he was driving up the wrong side of the road. I had to admit that all of us in the car were pretty much the same way, but I had the good sense to yell out, 'Pull up James, pull up, ya drivin' on the wrong side of the road. Ya wanna kill us?' With that, I took the car keys out of the ignition, and told him to have a sleep, sober up a bit and then go on home. He agreed and we all flaked and had a good camp on the side of the road, and then travelled home afterwards to Green Valley all refreshed.

The next mornin' there he was, him and Shortie, comin'

through the door with another carton of beer and I yelled at them, 'Get out! get out!' hunting them both out the door with their carton—I'd had enough with six days of celebration for one birthday!

I remembered the many times he'd come with me to talk for my two boys in the children's courts. He was a true tribal brother as he never ever deserted us when he was needed. One time in the children's court in Albion Street, Surry Hills, he was still talkin' to the judge, even after he'd let David go, and all the people were leaving the court! He was a real deadly old man, eh.

Another time I remember him was when we were having one of our little sessions. He got down on his knees and started croonin' 'Mammy, mammy, I'd walk a million miles for one of ya smiles, my mam-m-m-my'. He was a great fan of old Al Jolson. At another time he'd tried to stop me fighting with this Islander bloke who was boarding with us. This bloke used to get drunk and terrorise us by sayin' he was a devil worshipper. He'd come from Palm Island.

I think he had the devil in him all right, think he had two personalities, cause he used to change. He was eerie and frightening for my kids, and when he wouldn't go I decked him. Bam! Bam! I hit him a couple of times. James stepped in to try and stop us. He copped a couple of my punches instead and next day his jaw was all swollen. I told him, 'Ya gotta learn to duck when I start throwing punches, James,' to which he only laughed, holdin' his jaw.

Some good times we shared, and some bad times. He's always been there for me and mine and we all loved this 'little big man'. He will always remain in our hearts. I think my kids replaced his own kids from his first marriage, who had never bothered to look him up or help him. So 'Wandargie-way James', I was thinkin' as I nodded off to sleep.

LOST RENT

In 1982 I was living in St Peters. It was next to Camdenville Oval. The same battlin' to pay the rent and to keep a roof over our heads continued. Young Jeffery was in high school and Aileen my daughter lived with me, along with Patrick and Allo who worked when they could find employment. They were my two adopted sons. Nobby my eldest lived in Zetland and he often came over of a weekend to visit.

All week the house was spotless (Jeffo was off to school) and tea was on the table at five o'clock like clockwork. Old habits die hard! I was forever robbing Peter to pay Paul, which meant I'd pay one big bill this pension day, and the other one next payday.

Weekends were time for me to relax and go and have a beer. I'd do some socialising and it was the only break from all the pressures of the week, the pressures of living. Me and Aileen would go to the Clifton Hotel in Botany Road if we felt like dancing; otherwise we'd go to the Cricketers' Hotel across the road where all the Redfern All Blacks footballers drank. Many good times we had with our friends there—they looked after each other.

On one of those weekends I came home sozzled, got into bed and nodded off to sleep. The next morning the landlord was coming for the rent. This house was privately owned and Saturday was his calling day for it. I started to search in the zipper part of my bag but there was nothing there. Where did I put it? Surely no one robbed me at the pub. I remembered putting it in the bag. I sat bolt upright in bed and searched frantically, tossing things out onto the bed, and upending the bag. 'Fuckin' hell, some bastard robbed me!' I screamed, which brought the kids running to see what was wrong.

'What's up? What's up?' they all asked at once.

'My money's gone out of my bag, the rent money! The landlord will be here for it soon. Maybe I gave it to Brenda next door to mind for me; run next door and ask please Jeffo.' He came back and said that I hadn't.

I started to cry. 'What the hell am I gonna do?' The kids were comforting me and saying, 'Don't cry Mum, it will show up, don't cry any more, you know we'd give it to you if we had it, you know that.'

'I know yous wouldn't see me stuck, but the old landlord might kick us all out. AAHHHH! AAHHH!' I was still crying when I heard a car pull up outside and the door slam shut. Nobby was there saying, 'What's up, what's up Mum? Who hit ya? Why ya cryin'?'

'Someone robbed me last night down at the pub, my rent money's gone out of my bag, AAHHH, AAAHHHH.'

'Don't cry! Don't cry! I can't stand it when ya cry Mum! It's a good thing I got my Christmas pay,' he said, peeling 140 dollars out of his wallet. 'Now don't damn well cry any more okay? I can't stand to see you cry,' he added.

'Thank ya, thank ya my boy, I don't know what I would have done without ya help; we might have been kicked out.'

'Well he can't kick ya out now. You've got the rent okay. I'm going now, I've got some shoppin' to do. Bye now.'

'See ya,' the kids called out. 'See ya bra, thanks.'

Some months later Jeffo was helping me house clean, by doing the vacuumin' for me while I was dusting, and he was going over the floors real good. When we started on my room I said, 'Jeffo, I can't pull my old bed out, it's too heavy for me. Will you pull it out and give it a good goin' over for me?'

'Yeah Mum, no worries,' he said. 'I'll do it.'

He pulled the old bed base out from the wall and started the vacuum cleaner. Buzz, buzz it went, picking up all the fluff and dust. Suddenly he banged the nozzle onto the floor. 'Damn thing's blocked up, Mum.' With that he held the nozzle up to the light to see it properly. 'Oh gosh mar, it's heaps of notes blockin' it up. Heaps of money.' He started to laugh like a loonie.

'Well let me see,' I said. We started to pull the money out and counted it. I burst out laughing, saying that that was the damn money I thought someone robbed me of down at the pub. I realised then what I'd done. I got real cunning when I was charged up, and I must have planted it under the bed. 'Well I'll be damned,' I said.

'Well mar,' Jeffo said, 'I was rakin' up fares for the movies, so if ya don't give me ten dollars, I'm gonna tell bra about it, eh? What do ya say?'

'You rotten little goonum moogle, that's blackmail eh! If I give ya ten dollars, ya won't tell, okay? I'll tell him later on myself. Promise me now Jeffo.'

'Okay, okay, mar.'

The thought ran through my mind that now I could pay some of those damn bills. I'd tell Nobby much later but I needed that money much more than my hard workin' son. At that moment.

A few years later I told him what had happened and how Jeffo was gonna blackmail me when he found the money, and how I kept the rest for my bills.

'Mum, you're a real con artist. True! You old devil! Never mind, you must have needed it, old girl.'

NOTE
tita: sister

Mr Real Estate Man

When we come to Sydney town, from way out country way,
me and all me family clans needed a place to stay.
I tried to go and rent a place from Mr Real Estate Man.
But he took one look at my black face
and stuttered and stammered and tried to explain
(though he had places for rent)
there was none for me to gain.
'Sorry lady, no vacancies,' he said
though it was plain to see that he meant only:
for an Abo, like me.

THE CABBIE'S DISCRIMINATION

I'd just finished working on the footnotes about the Bunjalung
lingo in my manuscript and phoned for a cab to take me
back to Allawah hostel where I now lived. It was raining
cats and dogs outside and I didn't think the cab would be
as quick as it was. Beep, beep the horn sounded. I grabbed
my bag and ran outside and we were on our way.

'Bloody rain, rain,' I said to the cabbie. 'Sick'nin' isn't
it? Every weekend it rains.'

'Yes missus,' he said, looking at my bag of manuscripts
on the floor in front of me. 'What work do you do?' he
asked.

'I've just written a book.'

'You Aboriginal?' he asked.

'Yes, and you're Greek, eh?'

'Yes,' he answered. 'I hope in your book you tell your
people to get an education and not to take any more shit
from anyone any more. If you got education, you no have
to put up with people telling you what to do all the time.
I've been in this country Australia for thirty-five years and
I say to myself when I come to this country, I'm sick of
being called a "greaseball", "wog" and "spick". I'm gonna
learn English if it kills me. I buy a newspaper and I teach
myself to read.'

With that he started to rant and rave on like a cracked
record.

What an end to a perfect day.

Once inside I open up the *Penguin Book of Australian
Women Poets* to find this written by Aboriginal poet Aileen
Corpus. It's called Taxi Conversations:

the silence drones
the cars race
honking out a pace
the cab stops
the meter clicks
he turns to take my fare
but there i am no more.

why should i pay and submit
to cabbage minds like that
when i smell i can tell
a violent racist bait?

MARY FROM THE DAIRY

Allawah hostel at Granville is where I live. I became a tenant on 11 August 1987 and at that time it had only been opened and running since February of the same year.

This place was the first Aboriginal hostel for those of us older ones, who didn't have our own homes, and didn't want to live with our kids and become unpaid babysitters, and do our own thing. I'd decided that I'd done enough for my kids and from here on in whatever I made out of my life was gonna be just for me—no one else. I was gonna be only lookin' after number one. This might sound selfish, but that's how I felt; you can only GIVE for so long in life, especially when there were so many takers around, my kids included. So I thought I'd give up being a giver for awhile.

This hostel could accommodate ten people, eight permanent residents, and the other two beds were for respite care, for any of our Koori people who'd just had operations or were suffering from stress from nervous breakdowns and such; this place was real deadly and there were many stories to tell here. It looked like the 'good spirit' had pointed me in the right direction—it was a writers' goldmine, an untapped source of our people's true histories.

Here is one such story. The only other person here before I'd come had died, which left me the longest standing resident at Allawah. A couple of months after I'd been here, a few others arrived; there were two other women—one named Mildred had been going to the sewing classes at the AM Services for many years and the other was over from Cawarra women's refuge at Penrith. She was a woman in her seventies whose name was Mary.

She was deaf after two bouts of meningitis and had been

in a coma for awhile. I got to know her pretty well. I remember when she first came that she'd take off running down the street, with her stockings rolled down around her ankles, crying 'I'm goin' home to mum! This isn't my home, you can't make me stay,' not that anyone was nasty to her or treated her badly.

She did this quite regularly so the staff would have to run after her and coax her into comin' back. I found out from the co-ordinator that the mother she was so fond of was a white woman, who lived at Kogarah. She had fostered Mary out when she was about forty-one years old—Mary, you see, was an orphan and was raised by nuns in St Bridget's orphanage at North Ryde and then at St Anthony's convent at Waitara. When she was thirteen years old she was put out to service in Bundaberg in the cane fields of Queensland. There she had to milk twenty cows, morning and afternoons, and go to school in between to try and get an education. She also had to do domestic service as well.

These people were very cruel to her. They flogged her with a stockwhip to make her work and she took to running away from all the cruelty, but she was always caught and brought back for more of the same punishment. She told me once that she was pack-raped up there and then she was sent back to a convent at Tempe where she stayed for twenty-three years, working in the laundry, washin' white man's clothes and sheets for hotels. Because they couldn't find her family, she was eighteen years old when sent back from Bundaberg.

This white woman she called mother was a woman that fostered out children for holidays and such. Because Mary had no visitors or any tribal connections, she took her home one Christmas and it became a permanent arrangement as Mary was able to do housework and look after the gardens. Every year this family went overseas on trips, for holidays and the reason given for Mary not being able to go was a weak and feeble excuse that her mum couldn't get a birth certificate for Mary. Hence she couldn't obtain a passport for travel for her. They would have only had to get Aboriginal legal services to make enquiries. They would have helped get the necessary papers, or the Foundation for Aboriginal Affairs, but it was very convenient for Mary not to get a passport, cause someone had to look after the house, feed the chooks, and also look after the gardens. Mary was the 'Jacky Jacky' for them.

Twenty-nine years she stayed with her mum, who was only a couple of years older than Mary and had two sons who Mary helped raise. She'd leave the hostel every Sunday morning like clockwork, goin' and getting on the train at Granville and heading into town to go to church. She was a mad Roman Catholic ya see, and arrived back at the hostel before dark, about tea time.

Very independent she was. We were taken into the AM Service each Tuesday for the sewing classes, me and Mary and a couple of other ladies from the hostel. The ladies started her off with knitting, and she was in her glee. We got on famously she and I, and because I'd lost my mother, I told her she now was my mother. 'Okay Ruby luv I'll be ya mum,' she said with a big grin on her dear old face. Though we had some verbals too, me and me old adopted mum. There were potted plants throughout the hostel and one day I was comin' around the corner of the toilet into the dining room, walkin' real fast, when, Pow! down I went legs up! Someone had poured water on the damn plants and it had leaked onto the floor. Ruthy the cook came runnin' out of the kitchen when she heard the bang of me fallin', though I jumped up real quick lookin' around to see if anyone had seen me hit the floor and roll, because I'm kinda round built like a barrel. 'You okay?' Ruthy asked.

'Yeah, someone spilt water there,' I said.

'That was Mary, I told her not to water the plants,' Ruth added. 'You could have broken ya back,' she said.

Later on I was in my room, when I heard the co-ordinator rousing on Mary sayin', 'Ruby could have been hurt, don't water the plants any more!' Next thing Mary was at my door sayin' angrily, 'Thanks for dobbin' me in; I don't care if the plants die. I'm not watering them ever again!' and then she stormed outside to the verandah sulkin'. I was wonderin' what was up with her and I didn't take much notice.

Later on she was back at my door apologising to me. 'Sorry Ruby luv, I thought you dobbed me in, but it was Ruth,' she said, smiling at me real sheepishly. As she said that I hunted her and we never spoke for a couple of days. Oh she could get ya goin', this old girl.

She never referred to the hostel as home. She always talked as if the home she lived in with her adopted white mother was home. The co-ordinator told us at the hostel that when she first came here, they couldn't trace Mary's pension for a long while, because for twenty-nine years it had been paid into her mother's house account—so there ya go, she probably owns half a house, or better still the whole house! Mother never gave her any responsibility to handle or taught her or encouraged her to make a life of her own. The only reason she was here and homeless, like all of us tenants, was that after she'd been here eighteen months, her mother's husband had a stroke. There was a phone call from her mum wanting her to come home; she was so overjoyed at this news, she couldn't pack her bags quick enough. She had a beautiful suitcase with wheels on the bottom to make it easier for her, and nice clothes, not like the two plastic garbage bags she'd arrived here with, and only an old broken-down suitcase with a piece of rope tied around it to hold it together. Being here she had acquired a few nice personal belongings, whereas at mum's place she had nothing to show for twenty-nine years of servitude, only the gladbags and the old suitcase. She'd never even been to a hairdresser; the barber used to come to her mum's to cut her hair. When I took her over to Merrylands to my hairdresser for a cut and style, you should have seen the look on her face. Lookin' at herself in that mirror, she had the biggest grin.

The smile wasn't on her face when she came back from

her mum's; while there, helping her mother out she'd had a stroke herself and ended up in hospital for over a month. We were all frantic about her and when she was sent back to the hostel after getting out of the hospital, she was a very, very sad old lady. She realised that her mum couldn't look after her and her husband too and so she was very depressed, our Mary. She wasn't 'happy Mary' any more—she was 'Mary, Mary quite contrary'. She wasn't wanted, now that she couldn't contribute to the household workload.

We had a Koori woman come and stay here. She was a Queensland Murry woman, though she'd been living down here in New South Wales for about twenty-five years. Her name was Violet and she was a full blood. She and our Mary got on famously, like a house on fire. They developed a great friendship. Violet had just been discharged from the Royal Prince Alfred Hospital, and was on a kidney bag from the renal unit there. She used to take Mary on shopping trips into town and it cheered the old girl up. Violet had a whole ritual of changing those kidney bags and encouraged us other women to learn about it too. She was waiting on a kidney and had planned when she was a little better to go home to Queensland, to try and get a kidney off one of her five sisters. When she did go poor Mary was lost again; later on we learned that Violet had died, and Mary was very upset.

Though I tried to cheer her up, she'd follow me around in the afternoons when I was watering the gardens. I'd brought all my potted plants to the hostel when I moved out here. I had a portable grapevine in a big tub, and I grew a passionfruit vine and a choko vine. I was hosing these plants—even my old cunjevoi lily plant (which was nine years old and had big wide leaves and it was growing good here in the backyard) when Mary came out watchin' me waterin' them and said, 'Gee that's grown lovely,' pointin' to the cunjevoi lily. 'What's it called?' she asked. Mary's deaf so I looked at her and pointed to my ears, sayin' 'elephant ears'—she shook her head, not understandin' me. I tried to explain by giving her the hose and bending over and clasping my hands in front of me and swaying back and forth, and pointing to my ears—she finally got what I was trying to say; 'elephant ears', she said and I shook my head up and down. With that she looked at me with a mischievous grin on her face and said, 'Have they got wax in them?' at which I nearly busted a gut laughing. At other times she had sayings like 'I love ya better than beer, if it wasn't for you I wouldn't be here', or 'I saw a fly upon the wall, he left his card to say he called', or 'A peach was walkin' down the street, a chap went by and winked his eye, and the peach became a pair'.

Because she was diabetic as well, she had to take tablets after meals and she'd say, 'A pill for a dill', or 'One more crust and I shall bust'; she was full of these little sayings. She clung to friendships as she'd never been encouraged to go and get among her own people, to form any relationships or get married and have children of her own; and she loved children so much. Only a life of servitude has our Mary known. As she got older, she wasn't able to move around very fast and she got very frustrated because she couldn't do much to help herself. When taken to her mother's for a day's visit 'mother' would feed her with a spoon like a little kid, which made it worse for all the staff. They were told to encourage her at all costs to try and do things for herself and not become dependent on others. After a couple of years the co-ordinator left owing to something she had said. She was stressed out over our Mary's many demands— that wasn't the main reason, but part of it. Mary's world was dashed again.

At that time in the hostel the atmosphere was thick with backbiting and fighting among the staff and they gave the new co-ordinator 'curry'. They wanted to run their own race and take over the place, which the other boss had just let them do. And it was bloody terrible! They'd pump old Mary girl full of bullshit and the new co-ordinator copped the lot. The previous staff had left the hostel in a shocking state of affairs and had even come back on the pretext of visiting Mary to tell her things to stir her up! They kept the innuendoes goin' until the boss from the organisation in town got wind of it, and wrote an angry letter telling them to bugger off!

The old girl sat at the meal table whingeing and finding fault with everything. She told the new co-ordinator that she didn't like her and that she would never be as good as so and so was to her, which didn't do anyone's ego any good. Later on she settled down when she found she couldn't get her own way about everything.

Every time I was going to do research for my next book, I'd keep it quiet until the day I was leaving, cause she played up terrible on the staff, demanding to be taken to 'mum's' until I came back. That was impossible, cause 'mum' only tolerated her visiting for the day, and my trips were for a week at a time.

She used to get me to pull the facial hairs off her chin with a pair of tweezers, and she used to make a joke by sayin, 'Get the lawnmower to do my chin—I'm hairy Mary now.' I'd clean her two pairs of glasses for her too, one for television and one for reading. She couldn't hold anything firmly because of the effects of the stroke which she suffered. She's seventy-seven years old now and getting very unsteady on her feet, though her mind is as sharp as a tack. She knows how to manipulate people to get anything she wants done. When she's not whingeing about her aches and pains she breaks out with those little sayings which often left us all in stitches laughing: 'I tried those boots on down the centre, and ahemmm I looked like a maggot on stilks!' But she grew on you this old girl; you couldn't help lovin' her.

KOORI DUBAYS 3

My Daughters
Dianne Ridgeway: My Old Lady, 1989

I had five daughters; now I have four and Dianne Joyce Ridgeway is my eldest now. I call her 'My Old Lady'; her husband calls her 'Little Ruby' because she's fat and cuddly like me. She was married at sixteen, and she is thirty-five now. She has two children: Steven and then fifteen years later, a baby girl called Nikita Pearl. 'Pearl' after the sister Dianne lost.

Out of all my kids this woman is the battler. She's the home maker, gardener, chief cook and bottle washer. All my kids were close, but the three eldest were the closest—and she's the eldest now. All the worrying for the others seems to have fallen on her shoulders. She's like an old mother hen, looking after her chicks. Always out to help anyone she can, she's never had any of the luxuries of life, just the bare necessities.

Her eldest child is called Steven after his dad. He's six feet three inches tall, and a basketballer. He was the only Koori picked in an otherwise all white team to tour America in December 1988. Now he's doing his Higher School Certificate and wants to become an exchange student; he wants to go back to America and study art.

Money has always been tight for this family. But they'll make it, if there's a way.

Aileen Rita: my second eldest daughter, 1989

She was married to one of the 'Mutineers on the Bounty Mob'; his surname was Quintal. But the marriage broke up, and now she's divorced.

My two grandchildren of the marriage are still on Norfolk Island with their father; perhaps I will be able to visit them one day if the funds are available. Aileen lives in Bidwell, out in the western suburbs. As a matter of fact, all my kids are westies. With the exception of my youngest son, Jeffery.

Aileen has two children, Stella and Matthew. She waited a long time for a home. I call her and Jeffery the 'docile Libras' because they are docile until someone stirs them up!

But what I love about Aileen is that when I had major surgery on my stomach, two and a half years ago, out of all my kids *hers* was the last face I saw before going in to the operating theatre at eight o'clock in the morning. And it was the first thing I saw when I opened my eyes many hours later. She was just sitting there quietly, waiting for me to wake up.

I've never forgotten that.

Ellen Linda: my third daughter, 1989

Ellen was born in 1960. She's thirty now. Mother of four, one son, three girls; with my twentieth grandchild, a girl, was born recently.

I remember her when she turned fifteen and left high school, saying, 'I'm your only daughter without a boyfriend. No one wants me.' And then one day, a bloke named Ronny Nicholas came into my lounge and asked could he take my two girls, Pauline and Ellen, and their girlfriend Karen who was his sister, away up to the Entrance for a weekend. A bunch of teenagers were going, and he said he would take good care of them. He looked responsible enough, so I said yes.

Ellen was never able to say again that no one wanted her. They've been together ever since.

Ellen, out of all my girls, has the same personality as David, the second brother who died. Always laughing and going on silly.

I knew one day I would have to write something about

all my girls because they are great mothers and home makers, and I am so proud of all of them. But I don't let them know that, cause it keeps them on their toes, aye! They are forceful women, and don't put up with bullshit from anyone. But the thing I like most of all is they are endowed with the gift of loving and helping anyone who needs help. They are special people, my four women.

And by the way, Ellen has blessed me with my own namesake. Her eldest daughter is named Tara Ruby Maude. I'm thrilled about that too.

Pauline Anne: my youngest daughter, 1989

I nicknamed her Porkie Pie years ago. She's twenty-seven now, mother of three girls, she had them very young, just like me. And, of course, she's neurotic—just like me! This one is the peacemaker of the family—although she's been known to cause a few blues of her own too. She was a caterer at the Royal Easter Show for years, and then a home care worker. But now she's an Aboriginal Education/Liaison Officer at Doonside High School.

This is the one who is a real Jeng-Waller—which means 'mouth almighty' in my lingo. Always having a go at me because she says I favour the boys more than the girls! 'But I'm not angry,' she says. 'I know why you do it. To make us responsible for ourselves and our kids. And to be strong like you.'

Aye! She's pretty right about that. But wrong about me favouring the boys. Because I love them all equally and I'll always be there for them if they should ever need me. They all know that. It's because boys are more helpless than girls, aren't they? Every woman knows that. But my four daughters are all heroines to me, and always will be.

Harry Anderson, Ruby's father, in 1940.

Photograph by Elaine Pelot Kitchener

Evelyn Webb, Ruby's mother, in 1985.

Luna Park, 1968 — the same year that Pearl danced with the Prime Minister, John Gorton. Ruby's three eldest children are, *from left to right*: Bill, Dianne and Pearl.

Bill with some sailors.

Ruby's eldest son, Nobby 'Balugan'. (Balugan means 'hero' or 'handsome man' in the Bundjalung lingo.)

Ruby's little women in Fitzroy Street, Newtown in 1969.
From left to right: Pauline, Aileen, Ellen and Deanne.

Ruby with her eldest granchild Stephen Ridgeway,
collecting the Human Rights Literary Award in 1988.

Ruby on the verandah of the
Main Camp homestead in 1990.

At Box Ridge, after an absence of forty-eight years. Ruby
stands with, *from left*: young Gloria, her mother Gloria and
Ruby's Aunt Eileen.

At Main Camp in 1991, on the site of the old homestead in
Bonalbo. *From left*: Ruby, Shirley (Midgy) Coleman and
Judy Anderson.

MEMORIES OF MY PEOPLE

My nephew got married at Oatlands House on 14 October 1989. At this gathering of all our mob, I met my cousin Margaret again. She was there with husband Bruce and came up to me and said, 'Look cous, I've been home up to Cabbage Tree Island for a week and comin' back we called into Yabsley House. As we were bein' shown around, there was this big photograph of grandfather Sam Anderson in one of the rooms.'

'Gee, I searched everywhere for a photo of him for my book, but I didn't find one. I wish I'd known when I was writing the book, maybe they would have let me have a copy.'

'Yes,' she said, 'do you know that granny Wilson and another old full blood are still on the mission there at Box Ridge? And she's over one hundred years old!'

'Oh gosh, granny Wilson nursed me when I was little; I've got a photo of her on the mission with Mrs Hiscocks and old grandfather Breckinridge, holdin' a koala. I wonder if she'll remember me when I go back home?'

'I dunno,' she said.

I remember we passed Yabsley House on the way to the mission at Box Ridge and it is a guesthouse now. I remembered that I went to school in Casino with a Jean and Mavis Yabsley in 1947 and 1948. In Sydney the Minister for Corrective Services was Michael Yabsley and he was a member of the same family. It seems that their great-great-great-grandfather had sailed from Plymouth Sound in England in 1838 aboard the *Beagle* and was reunited in Australia three years later with his wife Magdelen. In 1843 William and Magdelen Yabsley moved from the Clarence River, where William Yabsley had pioneered a legendary timber, ship building and pastoral business. They had twelve children, three of whom died in infancy.

In her book (*Men and River*), Louise Daley recorded that by 1864 this remarkable man had established himself at Coraki. Around him was the beginning of the small empire which he'd created in the one-time wilderness. He also carried within his vision of what honest men could do, working together under different circumstances, for their own benefit. And after many decades, Yabsley House was returned to the family in 1987.

This information I found written on a brochure which Margaret gave me. Come to think of it grandfather Sam wasn't the only member of our family to work for the Yabsleys; uncle Sam, even Dad, and granny Mabel worked there too, and a lot of the mission folk had laboured on that property.

Then again I thought to myself, these early pioneers were in the debt of the Aboriginal labourers who helped build those big pioneer homesteads, for little or next to no payment. I thought the whole of Australia should appreciate the Aborigines, cause the whole place was gotten on the blood, sweat and tears of us blacks, and we never did get any recognition for what we did, ever, in this country.

I think the property on which we used to cut the ergot grass was owned by the Yabsleys, but I'd find that out when I talked to aunt Eileen Morgan. Aunt Edith Bostock told me that they owned all 'sandy creek' a long time ago.

Our grandfather's family came from Queensland originally, from Ipswich and Beaudesert; the Bundjalung tribe extended right up to Ipswich. There were two brothers, Sam and Bob Anderson. Grandfather Sam migrated down to Coraki and married into the Yuke family. That's where our ancestory began. The Bundjalung tribes extended from Ipswich in Queensland down to Tweed Heads then right down to Grafton on the Clarence then right back through Richmond River country and right back to the Tooloom falls and scrub. This was where the Bundjalung tribes originated from and there are lots of sacred places still there.

Grandfather was a drover and all the Anderson men were expert horsemen. On my mother's side, Mum's mother was a full blood Aborigine, and Mum's father was an Italian who owned a banana plantation in Billinudgel. He never raised Mum, granny did, and Mum's two other sisters were full blood, aunt Maude and Midgegay. I never did know Mum's mother's name, but she was from a mission at Tabulum. Mum was the eldest of the three and she was put out to service when she was fourteen years old. Ironically the first place she was sent out to work was Bonalbo, the town we were raised in. She worked for Tom and David Mills, and I went to school with their kids, though I never knew this until 1986 when I taped her before she died of Parkinson's disease. She was a good friend of my father's sister, Kate Anderson, and that's how they met and married.

I used to listen in great wonder when I was little to Mum talkin' about the olden times. They'd travel to dances, her and Dad, and when we'd go to sleep, Gwennie and me, they'd put us in the port racks of the old bus on a pillow, with a blanket wrapped around us. There we stayed till we got home. She used to feed us on bunya nuts, binging and bunihny. When she made custard she always put young crinkly peach tree leaves in and the flavour of peaches went right through it. She used to take us to a lagoon, and tuck her dress into her bloomers and wade out, feeling with her feet for turtles. When she got one she'd ring its neck and throw it out to me and Gwennie sitting on the bank. We'd put them in a chaff bag and take them home. There Mum turned them on their backs to roast them in the old fuel stove while we waited patiently for a good feed. The bunya nuts were roasted in the old open fireplace in the ashes and that's where she also made the dampers. And in my mind's eye, I could still hear the songs of my people sung in our language at family get-togethers.

Perfumes

Tomorrow, I'm going to be on a program in Carnivale, a festival that Sydney celebrates each year in September. This program is called 'disunities'. For the first time there will be Aboriginal participation and I will be reading with James Miller, who wrote *Koori: the will to win.* I was so excited about being asked, that I rushed around like a chook with its head cut off. Then I was invited to another festival in Melbourne.

I needed a haircut and style and also a zip-up carry bag for my dresses, to travel to Melbourne. I'd been asked to perform on a panel there too, next week on 10, 11, 12 of September. It would be a busy time for me, at this festival: it's called Spoleto. So I asked Ronny to drive me over to Merrylands, to get these things. I had my hair done and went to a chemist to get some perfume. I noticed all the different varieties and I went along using the testers, smelling them all, to see which ones were the nicest. I tried Australis, Lentheric and Marja and all the other ones, until I saw Cachet and a new one I'd never seen before, called Black Velvet; I was stunned! Here was our urban koori term for a black gin's vagina. With a chuckle, I grabbed it and tested it; mmmm, I thought—it's really good. So I bought the two of them, Black Velvet and Cachet. When Ron drove me home to the hostel, I hurried to my room and got into my old comfortable clothes and sat down on my bed, sorting out my things I'd bought. Margaret came into my room to say hello; she was on the three to eleven shift that day.

She spotted the perfumes and asked could she try them. When she saw Cachet, she pronounced it 'catchit' and when she saw Black Velvet, she cracked up! Me and her started to laugh our heads off about what black velvet meant, when

Mary from the dairy came to the door. We tried to tell her why we were laughing at the black velvet, by pointing between our legs to our private parts, because Mary's deaf! Margaret topped it off by saying, 'You better be careful with that black velvet because you might catch it.'

I nearly fell off the bed laughing, and at tea time we got the giggles too, talking about black velvets.

Jaymi's Dream

The phone rang at the hostel and someone called out, 'Ruby, phone call for you.' I picked up the receiver and said hello. 'Nan . . .' I recognised that squeaky voice. 'Jaymi, how are ya love?'

'Good Nan, look, I want you to write a poem about me please, can you make it up over the phone? I've got a pen and paper ready to write it down. You know, my daddy always wanted me to be a model. He called me his golden girl, remember Nan?'

Remember I did. My son. Her father. Died of an overdose in 1984, so with heavy heart remembering his loss, I came up with this poem, just for her. I called it 'Jaymi's Dream'.

Jaymi Annita is my name,
I'm a Koori and I'm twelve years old.
I'm long and lean like a mean machine
and one of these days my picture will be seen
on the cover of a magazine called *Ms Teenage Queen*.

There was a silence, then Jaymi's quiet voice saying, 'Daddy's gone now and I miss him very much Nan. Thanks for that lovely poem.'

Then the phone went dead.

The Way We Were

Travellin' back to my Bundjalung country
My heart was full of fear and dread,
Nearly all our old people were gone!
or most of them were dead.

What has happened to all our family clans?
Why have our people gone astray?
Learning all the white man's laws,
listening to what he has to say.

We've forgotten all our Dreamtime stories,
and legends the old people told;
we've lost all the sharin' and carin',
now all only for greed, or gain.

Our sacred tribal initiation's gone
The knowledge of our survival too.
White man has taken everything
our land, our hopes, our identity.
Now we have been dispossessed of everything
but there's one thing he can never take;
Forty thousand years of spiritual, cultural DREAMTIME!

The Reunion

The Anderson family reunion at Cabbage Tree Island mission at Easter time 1989 was one of the happiest I'd ever had, though at first I was worried about funds. You can't go anywhere these days without money.

I'd had several frantic phone calls from my sister Rita in Brisbane who was organising our accommodation. We could have stayed with any one of our relatives, though we hadn't been home for so long that we'd lost contact with all our mob. We opted for a motel and we'd share expenses. It was Ballina we'd decided on.

My agent phoned and I told her about the reunion. I said that I was broke and she said she'd lend me the money, because it was such an important happening in my life; it would be a shame to miss it. I thanked her after she said she'd deposit it in my bank account. 'You're an angel of mercy, Rosie dear,' I said. 'Thanks.'

I thought to myself, 'I hope it doesn't rain', as our city was overcast for days with a few drizzly patches, here and there. I went about booking my seat on a coach and the only seat I could get was on the 24th, Good Friday at 8.30 from Parramatta. I'd planned to travel back with my cousin Julie Anderson, who was my aunt Phyllis's daughter. But her baby was sick in hospital and I expressed my sorrow to her and thought to myself, 'Well old girl, looks like you'll have to go it alone'. None of my kids could come either because they were too busy with their own lives, and besides I don't think they realised how important this trip was, going back to see my people.

At times when I lay, trying to get some sleep, at the hostel, I'd think back to the days when I was little, and lived on the mission at Coraki—not that all my memories were good ones. I wondered if it had changed much or if it was still the same. I remembered a tennis court in the middle of the mission, not that us poor old blackfellas had the money to buy tennis racquets or balls. The whole area of the mission was made in the shape of a square, with about twelve houses, counting the old school house and the old wooden church. What had happened to the people; had they all moved away to find their dreaming? Did some of the old elders still live there? Old grandfather Breckinridge had a brigalow tree out the back of his house, where his chooks laid their eggs in nests he'd built for them; and there were guava trees growing everywhere, with ripening fruit. How we used to eat, and eat, until we had bellyache! Then castor oil was poured down our throats, UGH! Then there was the big common, down the foot of the hill, that filled with water when it rained, through which us kids waded each day to buy fresh bread; and near the old cattle dip, which smelled of phenol, where cattle were dipped; there used to be a big figtree with the juiciest figs and us kids raided that damn figtree every time we went past there.

I remembered it was quite a hike across that common into the township of Coraki, though when we were young, we'd run everywhere. We were full of energy, just bustin' at the seams with health, so alive and happy, we couldn't wait to grow up! I wished I knew as much then as I know now! They are famous last words, eh!

Mary from the dairy, my old mate here at the hostel, came into my room and broke into my thoughts saying, 'How long ya goin' for Ruby luv?' Mary's deaf so I held up three fingers on my hand.

'I'll miss ya, but I'm goin' to mum's for the Easter holidays. I'll be all right, you have a good time with your people,' she said, leaving the room.

I hurried around getting my clothes ready; I only needed enough for the three days. I hated to carry too many bags as I had enough weight of my own to carry around. But I'd have to take my boomerang pillow cause I'd get a stiff neck without it!

71

The day dawned when I was set to go. I packed sandwiches and cool drinks, put them in the fridge, and rested up for most of the day. It was gonna be a long drawn-out trip overnight anyway! Beep! beep! a car horn sounded out the front and I grabbed my bags and I was on my way.

McCafferty's bus depot was right in front of Parramatta station. I had a while to wait and so I seated myself on a seat bench and waited. There were people everywhere, coming and going, buses to Adelaide and Melbourne came and went, and amid the roar there was the hustle of trains pulling in and out of the station. At holiday time, people were on their way home to spend Easter with loved ones; I thought about all the lost and lonely people, with nowhere to go, no one to care about them. Some were sleepin' on park benches, in empty houses and some were finding their consolation inside a bottle, drinking themselves into oblivion, day after day. There was the endless battling to find some comforts in this harsh city environment and my heart bled for these people, cause I knew first hand what it felt like.

The bus pulled in and I struggled to board it, loaded down with my bags. Nobody offered to help me, as the rain poured down, throwing a grey blanket over this big, lonely city. I heard the passengers talking amongst themselves; there were quite a few accents there. I nodded hello to my seat companion, and when she spoke and asked me how far I was going, I recognised the accent—there were about four or five Yanks on board, and it made quite a mix, with all the ocker Aussie slang.

I dozed on and off for awhile, the music from the video making me real drowsy. The bus pulled into towns along the way and picked up other passengers, allowing a few minutes for the smokers to have a few puffs. I used these stops to go to the loo—those tiny pigeonholes on the bus were no good to me, I was a robust women ya see and I was frightened that I'd get stuck in them, eh!

I never tired of looking out the windows. The lights of little farmhouses in the distance showed up, making me remember my past bush life, making me melancholy, reminding me of days gone by. How happy I was then, in the bush.

It was six o'clock when I woke up and I realised I was in Bundjalung territory. We passed Woodburn and I craned my neck and looked hard through the window. We were now close to where Cabbage Tree Island was. I thought I might be able to see the old wharf, to which years ago we came by bus. We used to stand on that wharf, put our hands over our mouths and call out 'Bring the boat oooverr!' It was a good eight hundred yards across, and we waited patiently while they rowed over to get us. That had all changed now; they'd built a bridge over the back channel a few years ago.

As we passed Wardell, I saw the Ballina signpost and knew we'd be pulling in soon. I started to get worried— what if Rita isn't there to meet me? I wouldn't know what to do. The driver called out, 'We are pulling in for our breakfast stop now ladies and gentlemen.' It was showering too and I hurried down the aisle to ask the driver whether this was the bus depot or whether there was another one in the main drag of Ballina.

'I'm sorry lady, I don't know! I've only been on this run for a few days, and this is the only stop at Ballina,' he said.

Just then through the open doorway, Rita called out, 'Here I am old girl.'

'Just as well you're here,' I said, smiling. The driver got my bags out of the bus, Rita bundled me into her little car and introduced me to her Gubba girlfriend, whose name was Dawn. She'd come down from Brisbane with her. In a few minutes we were in Cherry Street, turning into the driveway of the motel called the El Rancho motor inn. It looked good and our room was number 18. It had one double and a single bed, a television, toilet and shower recess, and Rita had already stocked the fridge with goodies.

'I've ordered breakfast for all of us sis, bacon and eggs okay?' she asked.

'Great, I'm starved, but I'll have a shower first,' I said.

'Yeah, go ahead sis, you might want to lay down for a bit too, eh? Or you wanta have a look around?' she asked.

'I'll be okay after a shower and a bit of tucker in my belly; I'm dying to see Cabbage Tree Island,' I said.

We parked ourselves at the table and filled our bellies up. Dawn, Rita's mate, was a divorced woman too, who had a grown-up family like us, grandkids too. Her husband was a policeman, who'd run off with a younger woman. We laughed about how she, Rita, and me were all discarded women, though we never let it bother us any.

About ten o'clock we were back in the car, heading back to Cabbage Tree Island mission. 'Rita, I couldn't see the old wharf back up near Wardell, where we used to wait for the boat.'

'No,' she answered. 'It's all covered up now, the mangroves have grown over it, you can't see it but there's a back road I'll show you.'

'Darn weather! I wish it would fine up, though I know it's raining because it's the first time we've been here since we were kids. I'll bet we get blamed for bringin' the rain too!' I added. Rita laughed loudly.

We turned off the Pacific Highway, and came to a signpost indicating that Goonellabah was 26 kilometres to the right and straight ahead was Cabbage Tree Island. The road was getting narrower and narrower. We turned sharp left, crossing a small wooden bridge flanked by cane fields. I gazed out the window, while we bumped, bumped along, thinking back to when I was little. Dad had taken me along with a cane-cutting crew and my job was to boil the billy, and keep the fire stoked for all the cane cutters. I remembered how I used to get the cane knife to cut a stick of cane to chew on and how sweet it was. I'd bite the outer strips off, so I could chew on the sweet pith inside. Memories, all those memories of a time long ago.

Rita's voice brought me back. 'Here's the turn-off Ruby. Look, here's the bridge they built over the back channel,' she said. My eyes focused on the bridge. We used to row across here to buy lollies from an old Indian woman called Mrs Singh who had a caravan with wheels that was pulled along by a draughthorse. On crossing the bridge I saw aunt Winnie's house where uncle Bob had died a long time ago. There was a caravan in the backyard and I noticed that all the houses were raised up on steel frames. I knew why. When that damn old Richmond River flooded, LOOK OUT!

I was nearly in tears as we drove past the hall and the church, in the middle of the island. It was the place that I'd witnessed that cricket match in 1947 when I was thirteen years old, between grandfather Sam Anderson and his three sons. My father was the eldest of the family and I could still hear grandfather calling out, 'Come on goodfullas, play ya old dad cricket, come on.' My eyes started to mist over remembering all this. I could still remember the first time I'd seen dad drunk ever was that Christmas. We could see the old schoolhouse on a rise and Rita and me started talkin' all at once. 'That's where the boathouse and wharf was, in back of the old school.' We got out to have a better look but there was nothing there now; mangroves had grown over everything. Getting back in the car we looked towards the nearest house and saw this woman with long hair watching us. Rita said, 'Gee, that looks like Dugan Marlowe's missus. Edna, isn't it Ruby?'

I looked. 'Yep that's her. Hey Edna, come here mate,' I called out.

She saw who we were, and she came running calling out, 'Ruby, and Rita, I heard yous were comin'.' She swung her arms around our necks, nearly chokin' us, and cried, 'I can't believe it's really you two, it's wonderful,' she said. We hadn't seen her for a long time and she'd lost her hubby. A baby's crying could be heard comin' from her house. 'I'm babysitting my granddaughter, my daughter's shopping, I'd better go, I'll see yous down at the hall later on, bye now,' she called out as she hurried away.

Driving back we passed the church and hall and we were

trying to remember who lived in what house. Rita stopped the car in front of aunt Winnie's house. We wanted to meet all our cousins so I called out, 'Auntie Winny, are you there?' A grey-headed woman came out on to the landing above us. 'Don't you know us auntie?' I asked. 'We're your nieces, Ruby and Rita Anderson, can we come up?'

'Oh gee!' she gasped. 'Yes, come up, come up you two girls.' We climbed the stairs, planting a kiss on her cheeks. I gazed in wonder at her cause she hadn't changed, except for getting greyer, and looked exactly as I remembered her.

Her children came into the room, only they weren't children but grown-up people. Some we knew, some we didn't. We went about introducing ourselves while aunt Winnie chain-smoked. 'Everyone's gonna be at the hall, there's a big mob there already, from Brisbane,' they told us.

'Yes,' auntie said, 'and everyone will be here later on.'

'We're gonna go and get a good feed of fresh fish. We'll come back later auntie,' we said, leaving the house and going down the stairs and getting into the car.

On the road going back, after we crossed the little bridge, we had to move over to one side of the road, cause it was real narrow. There was this little red car heading towards us, goin' towards the mission. 'Wait a minute Rita, they said that cousin Judy's got a little red car, might be them, eh!' The car sped past us and we caught a glimpse of our two cousins, Midge and Judy. Rita blew the car horn real loud and the car came to a halt, and backed back; it was them! We were out of the car cuddling and kissing each other, wiping the tears from our eyes as it had been ages since we were all together. 'We're going to get a good feed of fresh fish; they told us that there's a good shop outside Ballina, eh.'

'Yes,' Judy said, 'it's the best one around.'

'Yeah,' Rita said, 'we had it last night for tea, me and Dawn.'

'Okay, we'll see yous back at the hall afterwards,' they called out as we drove away.

Rita was still raving about the fish, so I said, 'Shut up Rita, ya making me hungrier by the minute; come on, drive faster so I can taste it for myself.' Dawn was laughing at us always thinkin' about our bellies, and fillin' 'em up! The rain was still drizzlin' down making everything miserable, but it couldn't dampen our spirits or joy at being in our own territory again.

Pulling into the garage next to that deadly fish shop we filled the car up, while Rita went to order for us. 'Buy plenty Rita, cause I could eat a horse and cart, and chase hell out of the driver too,' I called.

'Don't forget the lemons,' Dawn added.

While she did that, I went next door and bought some fruit and soft drinks. I spotted those little Easter eggs with cream in them and I bought one each. 'These will do for desert,' I said to Dawn.

'Forget the diets, it's Easter time eh,' she laughed and answered 'why not'. Rita came back with this parcel of fish with all the trimmings and we drove back to our motel with the rain still pelting down.

We could hardly see the roadway, it was raining so hard. 'Let's not bother goin' upstairs Rita—takes up too much time. Pull in under the car park of the motel and we'll spread it out on the bonnet of the car and bog into it there.'

'Okay,' she said, 'that will save some time eh and then we'll head straight back—all right with you Dawn?'

'Anything's fine with me,' she answered.

The towel was spread out on the bonnet of the car, Rita opened the parcels of fish, scallops, lemons and chips, and we tucked into it ravenously. It was delicious. After finishing the meal, we washed our hands at a tap there in the car park and then we headed back to the mission and to the reunion.

Back on the mission, we went straight to the large hall. There were cars everywhere and even a couple of buses, though it was still drizzling with rain. It sure didn't dampen anyone's spirits. There was a lot of laughter and singing coming out of the hall, and the sound of guitars strumming along.

We opened the car doors and stepped out to go inside. Someone called out 'Ruby, Ruby' and swung their arms around my neck. It was my cousin Christie Bolt's missus, Margaret. She said, 'I glad to see ya sister,' and she cuddled Rita too. We introduced Dawn, and went into the hall. There were kiddies everywhere and lots and lots of people. They all came over to greet us, all our mob! The tears were flowing everywhere. Dad's only remaining family member, aunt Eileen Morgan, was there along with all our cousins and our mums. Full blood sister auntie Maude (I was named after her) was there too. You could smell the chops and sausages being barbecued, tables were set up all over the hall loaded with goodies and the little jarjums were having a great time—everyone was.

Cousin Judy, Midge, and Doug came over to yarn, catchin' up on all the years we'd been apart. It was just damn wonderful. Keith Morgan, aunt Eileen's son, said prayers to kick off the celebration and thanked everyone for coming. The guitars started to play and different ones got up to sing. I was surprised how religious all the older ones were— those missionaries had done a good job of converting our people who they thought were only heathens anyway.

The songs were old hymns we remembered from Sunday school like 'Rock of Ages' and 'Old Rugged Cross'. They sounded like the voices of angels, they were so good. They called out to aunt Eileen, 'Come on mother Morgan, we've got the gum leaves.' Auntie Eileen played the gum leaves, aunt Maude sang, and Grace Williams played the mouth organ. I was dumbfounded that they called aunt Eileen an elder of the Bundjalung people.

I asked cousin Tubb (that was his nickname, though he was named Henry after our dad), 'Where's ya brother Plonky?' Bruce was his name.

'He should be here and he's joined the God squad too!' Me and Rita burst out laughing.

Names eh! We all had nicknames—everyone was being introduced to each other over the loud microphone and the big reunion cake was bought in and placed on the table. Aunt Eileen and the other elder from the Queensland branch of the Anderson family, Mona, held the knife, cutting the cake together. The applause was nearly deafening.

Afterwards everyone tucked into the food but we were still full up, Rita, Dawn, and me. I sat next to aunt Eileen and when I glanced at her from different angles, I could see our dad, uncle Sam, and aunt Phyllis in her face. What a strong resemblance she had to each of them— it was eerie.

'How come you never mentioned me in your book niece? I read it right through and you never mentioned me once!' Her question took me by surprise and I remembered that I hadn't mentioned her at all—how embarrassin'!

'Never mind aunt,' I said, 'you're gonna have a starring role in my next one, okay?'

'All right niece,' she answered, joy showing in her dear old face.

People called out to each other across the room, eggin' each other on to sing songs. Sally Anderson, our cousin, was the first. She sang regularly at a pub in Mt Druitt in the western suburbs of Sydney. Her voice was strong and powerful, but nice to listen to. Then her brother Dougie got up and sang an old Koori song called, 'Cutta Rug'. Everyone went wild and began singin' along with him. The old hall echoed loudly with all the vibrations from the singing, handclapping and whistling that went on inside. It really shook the rafters and the jarjums were jostling each other to get a better look at everything going on.

Good thing I bought my camera with me and my small recorder so that I'd have happy memories of this turnout with all my mob. As the night threw a dark blanket over the skyline, it was getting late. The older ones and children started to head off for their homes and the younger ones were helping the older ones; I knew why! I'd seen some of them bringing cartons of beer, and a few wine casks. They had respect enough not to touch it until the elders left. You didn't see that kind of respect much in this land today and it made me so proud of all of them. It was a deadly reunion, and our Bundjalung lingo could be heard everywhere. We mingled with everyone, then said our goodnights, because we were real tired. It had been a hectic day and I was ready for the cot. It was a ten-mile drive back to the motel.

'I'll pick you up tomorrow Margaret,' Rita said to our cousin. She was coming to Coraki tomorrow, to show us where grandfather Sam was buried. All our family had been born at Coraki, the older ones I mean, Dad's brothers and sisters.

Outside the rain was still drizzling but I was hoping it would be fine tomorrow, though it didn't look like it. When we reached the motel, I crawled into my nightie and went sound asleep, out like a light.

A knocking on the door next morning woke us up. It was room service with brekkie. 'Come on, get up, get up! ya sleepy-heads,' I yelled. I pulled the blanket off Rita.

'Okay, okay, we're awake ya loud mouth Ruby,' she said.

'Come on or I'll eat the lot,' I said, rumbling them.

Dawn put the jug on for coffee and we sat down and ate our bacon and eggs in silence. I don't think the two girls were fully awake yet. In turn we showered and dressed. I opened the sliding door which led on to the balcony and cussed under my breath, because it was still drizzling. Will it ever end? Rita broke into my thoughts. 'It's nearly ten sis, we'd better be off okay. Big day today,' she added.

'Yeah, another big day,' I said. 'Let's go.'

From the balcony I noticed a pool, but it was no good to us with all this damn rain, I thought. The whole lot of the motel was beautiful—potted plants everywhere, palm trees and real nice gardens all around the place. 'We'd better take cardigans, we won't be back till late sis,' I said.

'Yeah we'd better,' she answered. We filed downstairs, into the car and out onto the roadway calling out 'Coraki, here we come.'

I turned to Dawn and asked, 'Are you having a good time meeting all our mob?'

'Yes,' she said, 'there's a big crowd of them.'

'Yeah,' Rita added, 'we got our own tribe.'

'From all this running around here, I'll have to go back home to Granville, and go leg up!' I said. There was much chucklin' from those two.

'I'd only be worrying about the kids if I stayed home,' said Dawn.

'Yes, we always worry about our kids when they're babies, and when they're grown up we still worry about them. That's the joy of motherhood,' Rita said, kicking the motor over. We were now on our way back to the island, to pick cousin Margaret up.

Into Ballina we went to get film for the camera and then we headed back to the island. We had hoped to find a bookshop open in Ballina as I'd heard that someone had written something about our grandfather Sam the cricketer. Though it was Easter time, barely anything was open at all.

While we were in Ballina I was thinkin' back to when I was about eleven years old, living at home in Bonalbo. Mother Nell had a sister named Mary Hinnett who lived in Ballina. At one time she was very sick and mother Nell asked me if I'd go and stay with her awhile. She was bedridden and couldn't see to herself and needed someone to do messages for her.

I enjoyed my stay there; it was right near the beautiful beaches. I was enrolled in the nearest school, which was a convent, close to aunt Mary if she needed me. I must have been there for about six months, when she got so sick that she hired an ambulance to take us home to Bonalbo. Poor aunt Mary died not long after we got back home. I got to like her very much and I missed her very, very, much.

My memories of Ballina were good ones. I used to go to Shelly Beach and collect all these lovely shells, sit on the wharf watching the boats going by and watch the crowds

of people fishing off that wharf. I saw the biggest flathead caught there—it was nearly as big as me.

I remembered the ride home in the ambulance to Bonalbo, when I gazed through the window, lookin' out at the country side in the Richmond Ranges, which we had to cross before we got to Bonalbo. Rita's voice brought me back from my reverie. 'There's a bookshop open, get the umbrella out sis, we'll get real soaked before we get there.' I grabbed the umbrellas. 'Wait in the car Dawn, won't be long,' she added. We hurried as fast as we could across the road, us two big robust women. They didn't have the book about grandfather. They said it would be in the library.

Back we went onto the Pacific Highway, on towards Cabbage Tree Island, to pick up cousin Margaret. There were miles of cane fields on either side of the road, some just ready to burn off before cutting, and everything was so waterlogged, because of all the darn rain. 'Ho-hum!' It was real boring the rain, only thing it was good for was ducks and the gardens. We were at the little bridge again, going onto the island. 'Where was Margaret staying, Rita?' I asked.

'At auntie Fanny Bolt's place,' she answered. 'I know where it is,' she added, 'it's the third house on the left of the school'. We drove past the church, the school, then turned right and pulled up outside the third house. Rita blew the car horn real loud and we sat and waited. Koori people were comin' out of their houses to see what was goin' on. Margaret was up a few doors visiting some people and when she saw the car, she came hurrying to get her bag. She was going to be dropped off at her sister-in-law's home in Casino, after we'd been to the mission. Her sister-in-law was my best mate in high school. I hadn't seen her for years too.

Rita went and helped her with her bags. She got into the back with Dawn. Rita kicked the motor over and backed back. Next thing we were in a big ditch and Margaret got out and called out to her brothers, who ran over and lifted the small car out of the ditch. 'Thanks boys,' Rita called out to them shamefaced. As we drove out of there, I looked towards aunt Winnie's house and could only see one of the cousins. I waved as we drove past, onto the bridge again. We passed all those cane fields again, until we were back on the Pacific Highway, heading for Wardell.

The car started to miss a few beats. Put! put! put! it went like an old worn-out heart. Put! put! it went when she revved it. We looked at each other. 'Oh no! not engine trouble,' Rita wailed. 'I just spent 600 bucks getting a new motor in it.'

'Maybe it's a block in the carbie,' I said.

Dawn piped up saying, 'It might be the fan belt.'

'We'll get it checked out soon as we find a garage open,' Rita said.

We were coming into Broadwater. Rita went in and bought some scratch lottos, but didn't win anything. We were off again travelling steadily and it was still drizzling rain. There was water everywhere and the next little township was Woodburn, where there was a big bridge over the river. It would take us across to Bungawalbin, then Coraki.

There was nice long grass growing and good stock food. Some of the little farmhouses on the side of the road were deserted. They had huge haysheds and old milking stalls too. I thought to myself that if I ever get enough money, I'd buy one of these old farmhouses. Although they were isolated and lonely lookin' places, it would be a good place to get away from the city, with its hustle and bustle.

Crossing the bridge, we were travelling along when a car horn sounded. This little red car sped past, pulling up in front of us. 'It's Judy,' I said. 'Wonder what's up.'

She got out of the car and ran back to us and said, 'Where are yous goin'? You were all invited to lunch at Teena's place, remember?'

Rita said, 'We damn well forgot all about it.'

'Come on, she's waiting for yous, got everything ready too,' Judy said.

'You lead the way, we'll follow you,' Rita said and we turned the cars around and headed back to Evans Head.

Evans Head was the place that we used to come to in the forties. On Boxing Day at about four o'clock we'd leave Bonalbo to spend the day here at the beach. We looked forward to it, as we were a long way from the sea. Aunt Nell and aunt Florrie used to spread blankets under the trees and us kids would be rippin' up and down the beach, throwing each other in the water and having a great time. There used to be a little train which took you all the way up to the main beach. It was a good hike if you walked it. All the tucker left over from Christmas Day was packed in boxes. There were cold slices of pudding and cake, home-made ginger beer which mother Nell used to make. I could almost taste it in my mouth. It was delicious. Then we'd leave before sundown and travel back. All the little ones were sound asleep, exhausted from all the running around on the beach.

As we came into Evans Head, Rita called out, 'Ruby look! there's where we used to swim, it's lovely and blue.'

'Yeah some memories here sis,' I added. Driving through the town we crossed a little bridge, that took us on to the other side, right up to the point.

This place was really beautiful. Everywhere I looked I saw those purple flowering trees. We drove into a driveway where Midge and Dougie were out in the front waiting for us. 'Where do yous think yous were goin'? Runnin' away, eh?' Midge said.

'We forgot all about the lunch invite,' Rita said. 'It's Ruby's fault,' she laughed.

'It's not my fault, you were drivin' the damn car,' I said. They were all laughing at us.

Teena welcomed us inside. 'Gee, Bub has got a nice home. Is it housing commission?' I asked.

'Yes,' she answered.

'Well! well! Things are lookin' up. Didn't think Koori people would ever be able to live in such a posh place, without someone complaining,' I said.

You really have to have a picture, to see just how beautiful this piece of landscape was. It was on a point that jutted out over the sea, overlooking the inlet.

'MMMmmm! What's that delicious smell?' I asked.

'The girls have chooks and fish cookin', come in and make yourselves comfortable,' Judy answered. We seated ourselves at the dining table and Judy introduced everyone sayin', 'This is my daughter Teena, her hubby Eddie, his mother was Gertie French from Mallanganee and these others are friends too.'

'Hello,' everyone said to each other.

A huge pot of tea was placed in front of us and we all helped ourselves. All the food was brought out to the table. It was a terrific luncheon, that must have taken some preparing. There were four breams, done in sweet and sour sauce; two large chickens, that certainly didn't come from Colonel Sanders; home-made seasonings; all baked vegetables, potatoes, pumpkins, sweet potatoes; honeyed carrots, fresh garden peas; and two big plates of fresh wholemeal bread rolls, and boy! did we get stuck into it!

There was total silence because everyone's mouth was full. We offered to clean up afterwards, but Judy told us we were guests and to go and sit down and relax. Out came my camera—I had to have photos of all this mob. 'Come on, line up here,' I said. I handed the camera to one of Judy's girls and said, 'Here take a lot, cause us mob haven't been together since we were kids.'

'Yeah,' Rita said, 'and we used to spoil your mother, because she was the baby.' Click! click! click! went the camera.

'I'll go to the mission when you go,' Judy said. 'I'll show you where dad is buried too.'

'That's a good idea,' Midge said.

It was time to go and we said our goodbyes to everyone. We got into the cars and headed out onto the road. It only took a few minutes driving before we were back on the little bridge going into Evans Head, and then on to Woodburn. Judy followed us in the little red car. We drove in silence for awhile, taking in the countryside. It would be great to own some land up here in Bundjalung country, but it was only wishful thinkin' on my part. If I lived to be a hundred, I don't think I'd ever be able to afford land here, or anywhere else for that matter!

After travelling for about ten minutes the Bungawalbin bridge came into view. Rita called out, 'This is the bridge Ruby! The big wooden one, remember? When we came down from Bonalbo on Boxing Days, this bridge used to rattle and shake! When the bus crossed it, it used to frighten the hell out of me!'

'Yeah I remember,' I answered. I remembered that they used to call grandfather Sam the Bungawalbin crack because he was one of only two Aboriginals ever to get Sir Donald Bradman out for a duck, the other being Eddie Gilbert. They never did get recognition in Australia for their cricketing achievements. Anyway, I could still hear grandfather calling out, 'Come on goodfulla, come on.' I think those words always inspired me to do my very best at anything I tried to do and not to let anything knock me down in life! They always made me want to get up and have a go. 'Come on goodfulla, come on' was an inspiration to me always. He died in 1959 at the age of 79 and he was still playing the game.

Rain was still running down the window of the car. I watched, thinking would it ever stop! 'You're real quiet Ruby,' Margaret said.

'I was just thinkin' about grandfather and Eddie Gilbert— they must have been two grand old guys, eh.'

'Yes they were,' she answered.

I looked out at the paddocks where the grass was high, and the cattle were real fat. It was good grazing land; you could grow anything here. Some of the sweetest dry pumpkins and apple cucumbers I ever ate came from here, squashes and marrows too! Mother Nell used to scoop the insides out of the marrows and stuff them with savoury mince and bake them in the oven. It was good tucker, the best!

Someone said it was only ten minutes to Coraki from

Cabbage Tree. We must be real close now, I thought. Rounding a bend in the road, the country looked very familiar to me. 'There's aunt Eileen's home over there,' Margaret said, pointin'. 'They're all on the verandah, wave Rita and Ruby, wave!' she said. 'We'll come back later, cause it's gettin' dark, and we won't be able to see the graves if we pull up now.' We blew the horn real loud and coo-eed real loud as we went past. They all waved back, calling out to us.

To the left of the road, we came over a small hill. I recognised the church and then the corner shop. We used to go there from the mission, to buy things, in those long gone days—coconut ice, iceblocks, milk ones with flavourings in them and cool drinks (my favourite was Cherry Cheer). And we used to cash in our cool drink bottles or kerosene bottles and get twopence each for bringing them back to the shop. Memories, I was full of memories.

Turning left into a street, we came upon the hospital. It brought back painful memories of a time when my people had only one big room down the back near the morgue, with a sign which said, 'ABOS ONLY'. It was a segregated hospital then. We stopped to have a look and Judy's car pulled up beside us.

'Judy,' I called out to her, 'is the hospital still segregated? Have they still got that big ward down the back near the morgue for our people?'

'No,' she answered, 'though they are still very racist here.'

I thought to myself, some things never change. Passing the hospital, we followed the road around, until we were right in front of the cemetery and we were nearly home on the mission.

Coming closer to it, I got the strangest feelings. I was frightened at first and then eager to see this place, memories of which were only painful. This time though, I'd be looking at it through the eyes of a grown-up, not a child. Rita drove through the gate. I looked from side to side. There was a small church right near the gate. Judy stopped beside us and I got out of the car in the misty rain, then placed my feet firmly on the ground, the ground that they hadn't touched for so long. I remembered it as a big place but I was only eight years old when I was here last. In fact, it was really small. I looked for the old school and memories of sulphur and molasses being poured down our throats every Monday morning flooded back. I saw the long wooden tables and stools we sat on to eat our meals; the old belltower whose toll could be heard echoing across the common, summonin' us to classes; the old vegie patch, where we toiled, growing things, weeding, and digging with trowels; and the girls' garden which was full of flowers: gerberas, zinnias and roses, whose heady perfumes made us mission kids imagine we were in another world where all things were beautiful, and people laughed a lot and didn't have a care in the world.

It wasn't like I'd imagined it, the tennis court was gone! 'Let's sit awhile sis,' I said, getting back into the car out of the drizzling rain. 'I want to do some thinking.'

'Okay,' she said. 'I understand.'

My gaze took in the whole scene, down towards the common, but grandfather Breckinridge's house with the big brigalow bush was gone! His chooks used to lay their eggs in nests he'd built for them in it. I was deep in thought. Where have all my people gone? Where have our family clans gone? Where is our tribal heritage?

My eyes searched for the paddocks where once tall millett grew, for broom making. In the place where the old schoolhouse was stood a modern brick home. I wondered what lucky Koori lived in there. There was nothing so grand in my day! Those places were old wooden places, with wooden windows that were propped up with a stick! No running water, only tank water and that was very precious and not to be wasted. Guinea fowls ran around everywhere making a terrific racket with their loud calls, 'KAA! KAA! KAA!' In winter the frost was white on the ground, like a white sheet covering all; it numbed our toes, turning them pink, when we crunch, crunched through it doing an errand. I remembered crossing a ploughed field when I was about seven to buy some eggs from a farm over the back, about three hundred yards away. They gave me a billy can to carry them in and on returning across that field, I nearly trod on a big black snake. I ran to get away from it but I fell and broke all the eggs, for which I was belted and sent to bed without any tea—they didn't suffer fools gladly in those days.

From where we were sitting, I looked down towards the old common down the foot of the mission, which was on a small hill. When it rained we had to wade knee-deep in water to get into the town to buy fresh bread. Us girls would tuck our dresses into our bloomers, and wade all the way across to the other side, about five hundred yards across. When we got colds they dosed us up with eucalyptus drops in a teaspoon of sugar, and hot lemon drinks with aspros.

We had no toys to play with, we were too poor, us old blackfellas. We made our own games up! We played with bike wheels. We'd run with a stick in the groove where the tyre should be, until it picked up speed. Boy, could it go! Sunshine milk tins were filled with dirt and a hole was poked through with a nail. You could put a string or a fine wire through it, clamp the lid on it and Boy! we had a steam roller! We'd race like mad against each other and play marbles and jacks, with the knuckle bones of sheep! We were good at improvising—we had to be.

I remember the good times like goin' swimmin', and eating guavas. But I remember bellyache! Then rotten castor oil poured down our throats! UGH! I remember tryin' to learn how to row a boat, on that damn Richmond River and how when it flooded, LOOKOUT! There was water everywhere, huge trees were uprooted in fierce storms and were washed downstream, when the river broke its banks. I recall eatin' cobbra, a wormlike thing that lived in the dead willow trees that were waterlogged. Then there were the fruits, raiding the empty orchards and stuffin' ourselves! Eatin' plenty of fresh fish, mullet and garfish, swans' eggs and bunihny and binging. These are the memories that came back to me while I sat in the car, the others not disturbing my reverie.

I never did have the chance to come back! All those years ago I had a family of nine kids to raise, mostly on my own. Boy, they took some raising I can tell you. I did any kind of work I could get, fencing, burnin' off, tree-loppin', men's work!—anything to put food on the table for my hungry brood! Although I was a trained machinist, that was only for the city living. They don't have a rag trade in country towns, eh!

It was with the deepest regret that I never had the chance to come home, to bring my kids and say 'Right here! I was born right here!' My mum had all of us at home! No hospital deliveries for black women in those days.

'Come on sis,' Rita said, 'let's go. No good remembering all the hurts, besides it will be too dark soon to find the graves if we don't go now.'

'All right sis, I'm sorry for takin' so long.' I went right back in my thoughts then and she started the motor up and we drove around the square. I caught a glimpse of curtains moving. I knew our people were wondering who we were but I didn't feel like talkin' to anyone anyway. About five hundred yards back down the road we came in on was the cemetery. We turned left there and Judy called out to us, 'Not too far down this laneway. I'll go ahead and show you the way.' She drove past us and pulled up about twenty yards in front of us.

This was the Koori part of the cemetery. We are still segregated here. We went in silence. Through the gate the ground was real waterlogged. It soaked right through our shoes. We came to a small section. 'There's grandfather's grave, he's buried with his cricket partner, uncle Alex James,' she said, pointing. 'They were buried together,' she added. The grave had a marble headstone. It was all mouldy and wet and we could hardly see their names. We found an old rag, and rubbed the headstone so we could see the writing inscribed.

All quietly lost in our private thoughts, we sat at the graveside and looked at the names. It said, 'In memory of Alex James, died 5 August 1946 aged 72'. Underneath was 'In memory of Sam Anderson, died 23 May 1959 aged 79'. I could still hear his voice calling out, 'Come on goodfulla come on!' I remembered how when I was little, and real grumpy, he'd swing me on top of his seventeen hands stock horse called Kangaroo just to make me talk! I soon yelled, 'Get me down! get me down poppy!' Then Judy said, 'That's aunt Phyllis's grave over there and that fence runs right over dad's chest.'

'What!' Rita said. 'How come they did that? I'm gonna see someone about this when I get home,' she added.

'The land councils are supposed to look after these graves, aren't they?' I asked.

'Yeah, I think so,' Judy answered.

They were in terrible disrepair and the rain made everything grimmer. I whispered a silent prayer to the good spirit that looks after all of us. 'Please take care of our dead loved ones.' We then left the place as silently as we had come.

Travelling back to Coraki, I was gazing out the window, thinking about who was responsible for the upkeep of the cemetery, when I saw to the left of us big fields of paspalum grass, 'ergot' we called it. When the whole mission came to work years ago, they came bearing reaping hooks and scythes to cut the grass, they spread it out on big tarps to dry and us kids had the job of carting it from the field to the tarpaulins. The older ones kept an eye out for snakes and we worked week in and week out, even on school holidays, until we had the whole paddock done. It left our legs with these black spots that itched. When they were scratched they'd turn into big sores, and the old women used to wrap our legs with bits of torn old sheets or old stockings.

I often wondered what they needed the grass for and why it was so in demand. When it was dried, the grass was threshed for the seeds, and bagged for sale. I found out it was for growing lawn grasses. Anyway we rounded the hospital corner and pulled up on the side of the roadway. Judy was gonna be leaving us, to go back to Cabbage Tree Island, while we were heading the other way to Casino to drop Margaret off. She came up to the window of the car and we all clung together, 'bye bub', 'love ya', we called. 'I love yas, sisters,' she called and tears misted up our eyes.

'See yous,' Rita called while revving up the car. She turned on to the roadway going towards Casino.

'We haven't seen her since she was about ten years old,' I said.

'Yes,' Rita said, 'time goes by eh, doesn't it?'

Dawn was real quiet in the back. 'Are you okay?' Rita asked her.

'Yes, I'm okay, just a bit tired from all the travelling,' she said.

The car started to splutter again and Rita and me looked at each other. 'I'll get it looked at in Casino sis, don't worry.'

Dawn said, 'Sounds like a loose fan belt, might need adjusting.'

We passed through a little town called Coddrington and then Tatham. Casino was only about twenty kilometres from Coraki, rain was comin' down faster and faster, and my little short fat legs were being scrunched up in this little car. 'We'll stretch our legs in Casino sis, not far now,' Rita said. This miserable weather was giving us curry, eh! 'How are you two in the back?' Rita asked.

'We're okay,' they echoed. The next little place was Greenbridge and soon we'd be in Casino. The lights from little farmhouses in the distance, back from the roadway, made me melancholy.

Some of the happiest times I'd ever had were in the country, even though it was real rough, and rugged. My kids and me lived like gypsies when we travelled around the fence lines. We'd always get to our destination before dark, set up a good camp, unload the tent and the mattresses off the roof racks. Water was carted, and a fire made, out came my trusty old camp oven, and abracadabra! A big pot of stew would be bubblin'—memories, I was full of memories!

The lights of south Casino were in view. 'We're nearly there,' Rita said. Ten minutes of travelling and we were in the main street of South Casino. 'There's the road to Bonalbo sis, many times we've been on that road, eh!'

'Yeah,' I answered. We came to the bridge. 'What's happened?' I asked. 'It's not the same bridge.'

'No,' Rita answered. 'It's a new one, the old one got washed away in a flood.' I looked down at the raging, muddy waters—muddy, because of all the rain, I knew only too well what this old Richmond River was capable of when it flooded.

This town Casino was the place I'd done two years of high school in 1947 and 1948. I had fond memories of 'Tiger' Magee, my old class teacher. He gave me piano lessons. One day he'd walked through the assembly hall and heard me tinkling at the piano, trying to pick tunes out by ear. He showed me the basic scales, later taught me how to read music, but I always reverted to playing by ear soon as he left the room.

He taught us how to tan hides too. He'd send the boys to the abattoirs to get the raw skins. After we'd tanned them we'd make toys for underprivileged kids. He was a good teacher old 'Tiger'! We called him that because he growled a lot.

Coming into the main street of Casino, we looked for the Marblebar cafe and the El Gronda picture show. Where was the store where we bought three penn'th of broken biscuits? We passed the park where I used to sit and wait for grandfather, to see if he wanted me to write a letter to Dad for him, because he couldn't write. Where was the Rink picture show? Nothing ever stays the same, I thought sadly to myself.

There was a garage opened and the mechanic had a look at the car. It *was* the damn fan belt. We got it fixed then drove through the town to Johnson Street. This street was the main road to Lismore and we'd come in a complete circle from the Island. 'Stop at that house Rita,' Margaret said, pointing. 'I've got a surprise for Ruby,' she said. 'Don't get out of the car Ruby,' she added. 'She doesn't know you're here,' and with that, she went into the house. Then I jerried who she was talkin' about—my old schoolmate, Olga, her sister-in-law. I could hardly contain my excitement.

She came back with this tall, thin woman who was wearing glasses. Margaret brought her around to my side of the car and she peered at me over her glasses. She then coo-eed 'Ruby! Ruby! Oh God! I've been waiting years for you to come back. Wait there! Don't move!' she said, running back into her house, calling out, 'I've got something I've been keeping for bloody years for you!'

I climbed out of the car to wait. The girls were giggling at us two, and they were as excited as me. She came back with something in her hands, then held it out to me sayin', 'You remember the old oak tree we used to climb up and hide from Bruce in, down along the river? Remember? Well, it died a long time ago and I saved this limb just for you, for a keepsake,' she said.

'You rotten old sentimental thing!' I said. I grabbed hold of her and we were cuddling and crying all at the same time. 'Gudgie (that's her pet name I called her), we can't stay long, we only came to drop Margaret off, wish we could stay longer. But there'll be other times now I know where you are,' I said as I kissed her and Margaret goodbye (as did Rita). We were on our way again to Lismore and then back to Ballina. It had been a long day and we were exhausted.

We travelled in silence and were all lost in our private thoughts until Rita said, 'That was a terrific thing she did sis.'

'It's bloody wonderful,' I answered.

'It's a lovely gesture,' Dawn added.

I looked to the left and right of the road, trying to see if I could see Imerson's paddock, where all the cattle were kept for slaughter in Imerson's butchery. Straight opposite was where aunt Amy and uncle Pentland lived. They were the Koori people who I was boarded with to go to high school here in 1947 and 48. All that had changed now. There were more houses and industries everywhere and nothing left of the past—only the outlines of the oak trees along the riverside two hundred yards away.

Further down the road was the Webbs' place; this was the place where the man lived who ran away with our mother many years ago. I shook my head to snap out of those old sad memories. 'Play some music Rita please, it will cheer us up,' I said.

'Okay sis,' she answered.

'Not any of those tear-jerkin' ones of yours, it'll make me sadder.'

'Okay, okay,' she said, turning on the radio.

Darkness was on us now and as we travelled along, I saw the faraway lights of Billinudgel in the distance, nestled in the mountain side. The Italian man who fathered our mother was a banana plantation owner there many years ago. Mum's mother was a full blood—that's all the info she told me.

These immigrants and white settlers and squatters, who came to live in our land, played a big part in giving us Koori our degrees of caste. They 'westernised' our country and now their descendants keep blaming us Kooris for what their forebears have done to us. We didn't ask for the degrees of caste that they endowed us with. Today Kooris come in many colours and it's illegal to define yourself as half, quarter, three-quarter, one-eighth caste, or octoroon. You are either Aboriginal or white, depending on how you identify yourself within the community, or are accepted by it. The bureaucrats sure word things the way they want them, eh!

Those men who gave us our degrees of caste have a lot to answer for, though these things are swept under the carpet, just like our Aboriginal history, which is swept under the carpet too! Things like this white Australia didn't own up to so easily. They tried to hide their guilt but I wondered how they lived with this knowledge. Unfortunately they managed to live with it quite well! I think!

Coming into Lismore, we all started to sing to the music, to cheer ourselves up! One of the sporting fields we passed, I could remember playing vigaro and hockey on, when I was in high school. Then I started to chuckle to myself, remembering our school's war cry. We chanted it as we were on the outskirts of this town: 'Mum! Mummlegum, mummlegum, gum Kangi, hoppiji, cherriwarra, whipori, try and beat Casino high, Yar!' Rememberin'!

Rita and Dawn were leaving tomorrow, Monday, for Brisbane. My bus wasn't leaving until 7.30 tomorrow night. We all had our own ways to go in life but I was saddened by that prospect. I didn't like to say goodbye to loved ones.

We drove in silence back to Ballina where we had our showers and dinner and hit the sack early, cause the girls were leaving at seven o'clock. Though I could lay up resting most of the day, watch tele until my bus left.

Next morning the girls hurried around packing their things, and getting dressed. 'Time to say goodbye sis,' Rita said.

'Yep, well have a safe trip home you two. Rita, I'll ring you when I get home. Bye Dawn, nice to have met you,' I added, cuddling them both. I watched them through the window; they drove away blowing the horn loudly.

I rang room service, ordered breakfast, and lay back on the bed resting. When breakfast came, I settled in eating it from the tray, dozing on and off for most of the morning.

About one o'clock, there was a knock on the door. Who could that be? I opened the door only to find Margaret, and Olga, me schoolmate, standing there with a box. They said, 'We came to have lunch with you! Keep you company and we got that lovely fish too!' they said.

'Gee I'm glad yous come, I was getting lonely now the girls have gone!' They spread the food out on the bed, with me still in my nightie. We remembered old times and stuffed ourselves with this delicious fish. What a time we had, the three of us. They only stayed a while cause Margaret's plane left for Sydney later that afternoon. I hated to see them go. I thought to myself that there had been a lot of water under the bridge since our childhood days, and I wondered whether we would ever meet again. Only time would tell. I waved to them through the window, calling out 'Goodbye my titas, goodbye.' I lay down again, and dozed off. I dreamed of the time when we were kids, Olga and me. We would climb that damn old oak tree and hide from her brother Bruce, who'd chase us home from school, beltin' us over the head with his father's newspaper. How we'd shinny up that oak tree to get away from him. I could still hear her calling out, 'Look out Ruby! here he comes!' We'd be quiet as mice, till he went past.

The clock on the wall struck five. I had a shower, dressed, had some tea and rang for a cab to take me to the bus stop. I was on my way back to the big smoke! Though it wasn't smoke I was goin' home to, it was damn rain. There was widespread flooding everywhere.

DEATH, TAKE A HOLIDAY

Death! take a holiday and leave us Abos alone!
So that we who are left, can point at you the bone!
You've whittled us down in great numbers,
no one is free from your call! No matter if we be
red, yellow, black or white at all.
GO take a holiday!
So our lives can be full of peace.
There's plenty of time left you see,
For our numbers, I know, you want to decrease.

THE INDOOR BARBECUE

On 16 December 1990, I was packed ready to go to Raymond Terrace for ten days, over the Christmas holidays. It would be the first time I'd been to my son's home up there, cause they'd only been there about five months. After many dramas down here in Sydney, they were lookin' to get the hell out of the city to make a fresh start, and raise their two children, both girls, Jessie and Samantha.

They had lived in Rockdale for about two years, strugglin' to pay $180 a week rent. That wasn't countin' food, and electricity, and phone bills. Jeffery had about six trades, and had always managed to find employment. He'd learned spray painting for about two years and then copped out because he didn't want to go to Tech one day a week. He became a die-cutter, but he had his hand crushed in the damn machine. They'd sewn the top of his thumb to his index finger to even his hand up, but it always gave him trouble; there went his football playing days and he was relegated to coaching.

He'd gotten a licence, become a tyre-setter and got a forklift driver's licence. Then he tried panel beating, and later drove a liquor delivery van for Camperdown Cellars.

When he did get the settlement for his hand, they decided to get married. They'd been together for about six years and had the usual brawls and frustrations that go with the cementing of a union of two people—in this case one white and one Koori.

The wedding was a credit to Shellie's organising powers; she once told me, 'Mum, you know your son Jeff couldn't organise shit.' I had to agree with her on that but I thought, I couldn't have spoilt him for being the baby of the family that much, could I? You have to at least let him try or encourage him to. Anyhow wasn't long before all the funds were gone. They had to be billeted with other members of the family. Ellen first, then Aileen, and last of all they'd come to me in despair, because things didn't work out in any of the households. There were always too many kids, and no privacy while they waited for their housing commission home to come through. In about three weeks, they'd settled in a caravan park at Prospect. Although they'd applied to be housed in Gosford, it was Raymond Terrace they were relegated to.

All the dramas were behind them, Jeffery had gotten a good job for a big tyre company in Mayfield. Shellie and her girlfriend came down to pick me up from the hostel. My youngest daughter Pauline was gonna drive me up, but they were going away for a month after Christmas and her car had to be serviced. Shellie and her girlfriend arrived about 8.30 on the 16th. As I went out to get into the car, the girls carried my things. But it wouldn't start. I sat down on the gutter swearing, 'Bloody hell! Every time I'm gonna go somewhere, something happens.' Shellie ran to the hostel next door and got a young bloke who was studying to become a mechanic. He mucked about with the engine for awhile and hey presto the motor kicked over and was purring like a kitten. No, more like a roaring lion, cause it was a V8 motor ya see!

We were on our way, with nary a stop, until we hit Raymond Terrace, and the street where the kids lived. It was about eleven o'clock when we arrived. I snuck into their bedroom and woke Jeffery up and then sneaked in and looked at my two grandaughters sleeping peacefully. We had a cuppa and went to bed very tired and weary.

Next morning Jeffo was up getting off to work, as Shellie and Sandy from next door came in. They'd been up early jogging and they came in all worn out while I spoiled the kids. I was ordered by Shellie to sit on the lounge and be a lounge lizard. 'You're on holidays! no workin'!' Each day I proceeded to sit on the deadly sinky lounge, and doze on and off while I watched tele. The littlies were in and out the house goin' next door and back to play.

All the time I was there, I rested up; boy, was I rested! We went shopping a few times, me, Shellie and the kids, and sometimes we drove into Mayfield to pick Jeffo up from work. This nice brick home of theirs was three bedrooms with a yard they could lock the littlies in to play. I was in my element spoiling those two. Jessica was a real jengwallah and Samantha, who was more reserved, wouldn't come to me straightaway, but it wasn't long before she was crawling all over me. I was still a big kid at heart, myself, eh! I loved talkin' baby talk to them, teachin' them nursery rhymes, which left Jeff and Shellie in stitches laughin' at me. 'Come on nanny's little goonie bums, come on, show me ya hands,' I'd say. And up would go their hands! 'This little piggy went to market, this little piggy stayed home, this little piggy had bread and butter, this little piggy had none and this little piggy, said, "wee, wee, wee," and ran all the way home.' I'd tickle them, making them laugh, or teach Jessie, 'Higgledy-piggledy, my black hen, she lays eggs for gentlemen, sometimes nine, sometimes ten, higgledy-piggledy my black hen', or this one she likes the best: 'One two, buckle my shoe, three four, knock at the door! five six, pick up sticks, seven eight, lay them straight, nine ten, a good fat hen!'— at which they clapped and clapped their little hands in glee! Nanny was having a good time too!

Couple of times Jeffo went out to his mate's place, to have a drink after tea. I'd watch the kids while Shellie drove him out, and when she would go to pick him up. One night he never came home. He was hittin' the piss too much I thought; ya can't work hard, drink, and some yarndie too! It just doesn't mix. Besides he should know not to touch that shit! Cause that's how we lost David. Yarndie wasn't enough and he'd tried heavy drugs for the first time and it killed him. No bugger about that! Drugs was only a cop-out anyway. Jeffery would say when I air-raided him about smokin' that shit, 'But mar, I'm not David!'

On Christmas Eve we all piled into the car and went to look at a place called Taro to show the littlies all the

Christmas lights. It was a tradition the kids told me; all the people living in that place decorated their homes every Christmas, with Santa and reindeers, and nativity scenes. The whole place was lit up with all these coloured lights and it was really beautiful. People were coming from all over the countryside to have a look. They'd park their cars and walk through the whole suburb showing the children all the glorious lights. It really showed that the Christmas spirit still survived in some places in Australia. It wasn't all commercialism, though it must have cost these people plenty for the electricity, eh! Later on coming back to Raymond Terrace, we took the kiddies through the town to show them a huge Christmas tree all lit up in their own little township. I watched the expressions on their little faces—they glowed with joy.

On Christmas Day, we were up early getting ready to travel to Gosford to spend the day with Shellie's family. It was a good day. We had lunch out the backyard under beach umbrellas cause it was so damn hot. The food was laid out beautifully, me and Shellie's dad talked politics most of the day. All the family was there and the kids played cricket and it made a good day of getting together. Later on when it was cooler, we travelled back to Raymond Terrace, all tired out. Jeffo was sozzled, so Shellie drove back, as he'd driven down.

A barbecue was arranged for a Saturday, with Jeff's working mates. They were a good bunch and I was pleased that Jeff and Shellie had settled in and made some friends up here. The barbecue was gonna be held at one of the older workmate's place. Jeff called him 'Stan the man' when I was introduced to him. He shook my hands sayin', 'Oh! you're the writter! you're the writter!'

'Yes,' I answered, 'I'm the writter,' laughing how he had pronounced 'writer'. He told me he said to Jeff that Jeff wasn't black and that he was the real black because his surname was Black.

On the day we were to go, the car was acting up. The

kids had a new transmission put in it, but it still stuffed up on them. It once caught fire, when Shellie went to pick Jeff up at the mate's place, after a booze up. Good thing they had a fire extinguisher with them or it would have burned! Then they'd be stuck for transport for Jeff to get to work. Matter of fact the morning after it had caught fire, his next-door neighbour came in at 7.30 and said, 'I'll drive you to work, and get that piece of hose ya need. Me and Ken will have it fixed by the time you knock off work, okay?' How's that for good neighbours! You'd be flat out to find anyone to help you out like that in Sydney! It was twenty minutes' drive each day into his workplace, from Raymond Terrace.

Finally they got the car goin' again, with the help of his two young workmates, named Steve and Grahame who were brothers. They pushed it back and forward, till it kicked over. They had this little mastiff pup they called 'HD'. They bundled it into the car and we were on our way. The temperature reached 42 degrees and sweat was pouring out of all of us. The littlies slept most of the way and the boys pulled into a drive-in bottle shop, to stock up with tinnies. They had a big esky in the boot of Jeff's car, and I felt like celebrating so I bought a six-pack of Island Coolers, for me and Shellie. Then we picked Stan the man's wife and family up. We were goin' to a place called Paterson, over the other side of Maitland and we seemed to take forever to get there. We drove into a park beside the river, which had big shady trees, and picnic tables and stools. The river bank was real steep so Jeffery helped me down to sit under a big willow tree out of the sun. He spread a big towel out for me to sit on. The rest made for the water, with the little ones, who had their ears plugged up, to stop water gettin' in.

The place was crowded with people, families with all their kids, cooling off in the water. The little ones were being towed around on mum or dad's backs, hanging on for dear life! There was lots of laughter and jostling going on. I had to be content to sit under the willows, which were all along the river bank. It was a very beautiful spot; but a pity it was so damn hot! I had intentions of goin' into the water, but there were no dressing sheds here, and besides, I didn't want to go behind any bushes to change. It would be too much bother.

'AAAaaagh! Look out! Look out!' someone yelled. 'Snake, snake.' I looked in that direction, saw a big snake wriggling through the water, headin' straight towards the swimmers. PANIC! There were people grabbin' their kids, hurryin' out of the water. Jeffo had the two little ones further back away. BOY! I never ever saw a river or swimmin' hole get cleared so quick! People hurrying past turned to ask me, 'Is it a venomous one lady?' They must have thought this old black woman would know. But because I was without my glasses (I'm short-sighted) I called out, 'Nar! It's only a green willow tree snake. It's not dangerous.' Shellie came up the bank and asked me, 'What'll we do Mum?'

'Get a big limb, and hit the water, it will frighten it away,' I answered.

'Okay,' she said, and off she ran. But when she returned, I saw she only had a small branch with which to beat the water. Shish! swish! swish! it sounded. Anyhow the closer the damn thing came I could see that it really wasn't green, but brown, and they're venomous!

'Get back, get back, Shellie!' Jeffery called out. At that the snake headed further upstream, away from all the screamin' and yellin' goin' on. 'Come on Mum, bugger this place,' they said. 'Let's go, the snake can have it,' they echoed.

I didn't want to climb all the way back uphill, but if the bloody snake was still there I'd move real fast I bet! Jeffo brought the car right down on a bush road we hadn't seen. Soon we were back under the shady trees, the boys having beers and us women gettin' stuck into the Island Coolers. We had plenty of ice for the kiddies, too. Later on we loaded the drinks back into the cars and headed out, going back to Stan the man's place for the barbecue. Since he had not one tree for shade in his yard, he rigged up an electrical cooker in his kitchen and the smell of the sausages and chops and onions wafting through the whole house smelled real good.

They had fans going, and air-conditioning too, but that didn't give us much relief. I had to laugh though, it was the first time I'd ever been to an indoor barbecue. Jeff's mates Steve and Tom were playin' with the pup and calling out, 'Here HD, come here HD.' I asked them, 'Why do you call the dog HD?'

Tom answered. 'It's short for "here dawrg, hey dorg",' and I nearly busted a gut laughing.

'Ha-ha-ha, I'm gonna write a story when I go home about the snake that cleared the swimmin' hole and a dog called HD.'

They all had a good chuckle about that and said, 'Don't you dare, old girl, don't ya dare!'

Before we left to go home, I autographed one of my books, for Stan the man. I wrote 'To Stan Black, from a real black!' It left him misty-eyed. He thanked me and said, 'You old writter! You old bugger!' They were all good bush people, no bullshit about any of them, battlers like us all; they sure knew how to laugh at life through all its hard knocks.

NOTES
jengwallah: chatterbox
yarndie: marijuana

SHAME DAY, MY BIRTHDAY —26 JANUARY

I reside in an Aboriginal hostel called Allawah which means, 'Stop! sit down and rest awhile' in Aboriginal lingo. It's very appropriate, cause boy! I sure needed a place like that. I don't have a home of my own; I'm not whingeing, because there are thousands of my people like me, 'homeless'.

At all costs, the government's policies were to assimilate us or wipe us off the face of the earth; sounds brutal but it's the truth! This country was founded on a lie, the lie of *terra nullius* which means it was uninhabited, and I don't think our ancestors, the indigenous people, were invisible. Even those who migrate here are on a higher social level than we are; we are classified as the lowest of the low. On the tele, and in newspapers—though they only show the negative side of our culture, never the positive stuff.

This story is about my birthday; you see I was born on 'shame day' in 1934, though I had nothing to do with that decision! I was only 'a gleam in my daddy's eyes you see'. My kids had made arrangements to all lob here at the hostel. We were gonna have a picnic lunch on the verandah, so we wouldn't disturb the other residents.

Early on 26 January I was up, had my bed made and room cleaned up. I was watching tele, and also the wall clock, thinkin' that it didn't look like anyone was coming and that oh well my kids had families of their own. I thought I really didn't need all this adoration bit about birthdays. I was gonna start counting backwards after this one anyhow! Cause in three more years I'd be sixty! Holy cow! I was gettin' real ancient, eh! I glanced at the wall clock again which said eleven o'clock. I was feeling real let down, thinkin' they're not comin', the buggers.

A noise at the door caught my attention. I turned to see my son Jeffery and his wife Shellie, with the two little grandkids Jessie and Samantha. The littlies had a big bunch of red and white carnations, and Sam the baby was carrying a card. 'Happy birthday,' the littlies echoed, coming into the room. My old spirits lifted up.

'Oh! I thought no one was gonna come,' I said misty-eyed, kissing and cuddling them all.

They said, 'We got a call from Pam, and the others; they won't be able to come.'

'But,' I said, 'Dianne was comin', we had it all planned.'

'Come on,' Jeffery said, 'let's go for a drive. I've gotta pick up my hose and some tools I left at Aileen's place, last time we were down.'

'Come on, let's go, chop chop, Mum,' Shellie said.

I had on an old sun frock, cause it was bloody hot! 'Will I put on something better?' I asked. 'Cause it's my birthday?'

'Nar! That's okay, we're only goin' for a drive,' Jeffo said.

I grabbed my bag and we left the hostel just going on twelve o'clock calling out goodbye to everyone as we left. Along the highway, I could see takeaway places open and my belly was starting to rumble. 'We should get some takeaway cause it's lunch time,' I said.

'No, I can't stop, the traffic is too heavy, Mum,' Jeff said. On to Mt Druitt we drove, goin' through Dharruk heading to Bidwell and just as we turned into Acacia Terrace where Aileen lived, I spotted all the cars outside her gate—Ellen's, Pam's and Pauline's. I let out a yell as I got out of the car. 'Holy cow! Yous got me! yous got me! You buggers,' I screamed laughing.

I waved my fist at them, the back gate opened and there they all were, my kids and grandkids lined up singing, 'Happy birthday to you, happy birthday to you'. 'AAggghhh! yous all got me, eh! You buggers, all of yous sucked me right in!' They were all cuddlin' and kissin' me sayin', 'We got ya ha ha!' They were all laughing like buggery.

'Come on inside mar,' Aileen said. All the littlies followed me inside, coming into the lounge. They had the table set up with all the goodies, golden roast chickens—my favourite food. There was every salad imaginable, potato, Greek, with black olives, and Italian. WOW! It was mouth-watering, and there were fruits, grapes and wholemeal breadrolls.

'Come on, sit down here Mum,' Aileen said, steering me to a chair at the end of the table. 'Tuck in, go on, help yourself.'

'Want a glass of champagne mar?' Jeffo asked.

'Yeah, that will be real deadly,' I answered, tucking into the tucker. The older ones helped the littlies, who were having a great time.

Pauline came through the doorway carrying the cake which she'd made herself. It was chocolate, my favourite. They all gathered round me at the table, sayin', 'Come on, cut the cake.' They passed me a big knife and when I'd done that, they were clapping and singing 'Happy birthday' to me. The kids joined in: 'Why was she born so beautiful?' They also added, 'and fat too!' 'Why was she born at all?' they echoed, laughing. 'She was born to have all us mob!' I was thinking while the tears rolled down my cheeks, I wish I had a damn tape! I'd get all these buggers bustin' their goonums singin' to me.

There was a big sign up in the lounge, which said, 'No smoking'. 'Everyone that smokes, outside please,' Aileen yelled, 'cause Mum's allergic to it, okay?'

'Yeah,' they answered, disappearing out on the front porch, while I stuffed my face with the tucker and drank glasses of champagne. 'Who got all this stuff?'

'Pammy,' they said, 'she was the schemer of all this mar.' They gave Pammy up, they did.

Everyone had some cake, it was deadly. Then Pauline and Roberta, her daughter, entertained us with a comedy sketch. It was very funny, everyone said, 'Boo! Boo! Get off, get off or get on with the show,' so Pauline started rubbing cake into Ellen's face, then it was on for young and old. I laughed so much I nearly fell off the damn chair.

Dianne, my eldest, who I called 'my old lady', was getting tiddly and said to me, 'I'm gonna get all these bitches while they're all together Mum! I'm gonna give 'em heaps.' With that, chocolate cake was slapped into her face, and she was splutterin' and grabbin' some and rubbin' it into Jeffery's face. It snowballed until everyone's face was all chocolate, even the littlies too.

I wasn't gonna miss out. With my camera I was click, clickin', hoping these photos would come out. After much jostling and shoving they decided to wash it off, sayin', 'Come on, it's bloody hot, let's wash it off.' Someone got the bright idea of dunkin' everyone in the shower, first to go was Ellen, screamin', then Pauline, Roberta, then Aileen. Then it was Jeffo's turn, it took six of 'em, including grandson Steve, all 6ft 3 and 15 stone of him. They were draggin' him towards the bathroom door, with Jeffo plantin' his big feet, that we called 'aircraft carriers', firmly on the floor. They couldn't move him so they lifted him bodily. Oh what a day my birthday turned out to be. My sides were sore from laughing so much.

Pam was sitting next to me lookin' real pretty. The revellers came back after Jeffo was dunked. 'We can't wet ya Mum, cause you're the birthday girl,' but all the same, someone got the champagne and orange juice and poured it over my head. I was soaked anyhow. 'You buggers,' I yelled.

Pretty sittin' Pammy was next. They picked her up bodily, with her long black dress, and dreadlocked hair hanging down. She grabbed hold of the doorway, but was carried to the bathroom, comin' out drenched like a drowned rat.

I sat thinking after it was all over, this is the first time all of us had gotten together for a long time. Though I wouldn't change places with the Queen of England for what I was seeing in this house this day, there was so much love, and laughter, then jokes were being told and the more that were told the sicker they got.

Only two of my grandkids weren't here: Jaymi and Davy-boy, and Nobby my eldest son was in Berrima Jail. Never mind! There'd be other times.

I stayed with them until six o'clock and then Patrick and I got a lift home with Pam, cause I had to be down the State Library to hear Mudrooroo reading. Besides, I wanted to ask his permission to quote from his book (*Writing from the Fringe*) at my reading at an A.S.A.L. literature conference.

I was showered and dressed and ready for the taxi that was picking me and Patrick up at the hostel here. I might add, it was the quickest I'd ever gotten ready for a do. The reading was at the Library in the Glasshouse Cafe. As we entered I waved hello, to Muddy. After his reading, he called out, 'I'd like to take this opportunity to wish Ruby Langford a happy birthday.' I answered, 'I didn't have anything to do with my birthday date, but thanks, Muddy, for the good wishes.' Afterwards I left Patrick off down at the Clifton, and came home to the hostel plum tuckered out!

I rested up all next day then on the Monday I got a phone call from my two grandkids over in Busby that weren't at my birthday. One said, 'Nan, uncle Jeff's here, they stayed with us last night. Get ready, we're comin' to pick you up and take you fishing, okay?'

'Yeah, that will be good,' I answered. I rushed to get ready, I hadn't been fishing for bloody years! I was real excited. Jeffery and Michelle never went back to Raymond Terrace where they lived after my party. They had stopped over to see my dead son David's children, and spend some time with them. My daughter-in-law, Debbie, had taken up with another bloke after David had died. He was good to the grandkids and they had everything they wanted.

A car horn sounded and I hurried outside. It was Jeffery and Michelle, who picked me up and then went back to Busby to round up the other mob. We headed out to Bundeena, with the fishing lines in tow. We got bait, and the littlies had a good time splashing about in the water, while the girls went to buy lunch. This place was crowded and after lunch I spread a rug out on the sand and went sound asleep. So much for fishing, but it was a good day anyhow. I got ribbed about snoring loudly and letting the fish get away. Davy-boy and his little mate collected shells along the beach for me as I had a passion for shells.

Back at the hostel that night I was thinking that my birthday, 26 January (which us Abos call shame day cause it was the day our land was taken over by the colonists in 1788), had turned out to be the best birthday I ever had in my life. I'll have to send all my kids a little thank you card, for making it so special, and show them my appreciation. Now you know why I wouldn't change places with the Queen of England, for what I've got in my own backyard, eh!

NOTE

goonums: arses

WARDS OF THE STATE
An Autobiographical Novella
ROBERT ADAMSON

She sat on the mudguard and let her hair roll forward; black hair fell down her face, but she didn't care about the screaming going on all around her. She just wanted to keep moving, to get back into the car and go. Anywhere, what did it matter, as long as the road hissed behind her.

Robert Adamson's autobiography is a poetic evocation of his childhood and boyhood in Sydney and on the Hawkesbury River. It encompasses the teenage dreams — girls, cars and impending manhood — which drew him into the closed net of boys' homes and a criminal life. Adamson finds in writing both release and resolution.

'Adamson is probably the best lyric poet in the country.
He can write about the natural world more convincingly
than anyone else. But at the same time Adamson is completely
contemporary in his verse technique.
He is a sort of feral Mallarmé.'
JOHN FORBES, *MELBOURNE HERALD*